IN AND BY

Items sorted out of my experiences on the

Fort Worth Stockyards 1945 — 1955

Bill Sloan

Honey Creek Press

FIRST EDITION

Copyright © 1987
By William V. Sloan

Published by Honey Creek Press

Printed in the United States of America
By Nortex Press, Austin, Texas

Library of Congress Cataloging-in-Publication Data

Sloan, Bill.
    In and by : items sorted out of my experiences on the Fort Worth stockyards, 1945–1955 / Bill Sloan. — 1st ed.
       p. cm.
    Includes index.
    ISBN 0-89015-611-5 : $15.95
    1. Cattle trade — Texas — Fort Worth. 2. Stockyards — Texas — Fort Worth. I. Title.
HD9433.U5F677   1987
338.7′63620831 — dc19   87-26279
                                                  CIP

Contents

Aerial view of the Fort Worth Stockyards 1946. W.D. Smith photo.

Foreword
An Important Page of Americana

When Fort Worth was getting started there were two things that changed it from a crossroads to a city. They were the arrival of the railroads and the building of the Fort Worth Stockyards and the packing houses. In those days those things were what provided the important business and financial basis for today's Cowtown.

When Bill Sloan told me he was writing this history and explanation of how the Stockyards worked I was delighted. The Yards, as it was affectionately known, was peopled by the kind of people who appreciated opportunity and hard work and integrity. Integrity was the key that made the Yards a great place.

In these days and times it may be difficult to grasp the character involved in dealings involving millions of dollars, when a million was really a million, when the private treaty trading was man to man, person to person, and did not involve lawyers, auditors and all of those details necessary today. The buyer bid, the seller accepted or rejected, and the fantastic memory in remembering all of these transactions puts today's computers to shame.

Everyone involved in the Yards was quick on the draw when misfortune struck another person. While competition was fierce, the brotherhood of man scrubbed differences and disputes and when the word went around that someone needed some help all hands were at the ready, whether it was money or personal help.

There are those today who shun the title of Cowtown for our city. We feel sorry for them, since their problem is the fact they never knew the industry and they are doubly punished because they never knew the peculiar brand of truly great Americans who made the Yards different and great.

Thanks, Bill, for preserving these memories.

Ted Gouldy,
Editor, Publisher of The Weekly Livestock Reporter

Acknowledgments

Thanks to:

Deborah Lightfoot Sizemore, editor and agricultural journalist, for her expertise in correcting, refining and polishing the manuscript for publication.

G.G. Park for her work is arranging my random thoughts and ideas into a readable format.

John Stone, one of my favorite artists, for his pencil drawing "In and By" that is reproduced on the cover of this book.

N.M. Davidson, who did the drawings used in this book. The drawings were originally used in a pamphlet printed by the Fort Worth Stockyards Company in 1938.

Darel Hampton for the loan of several photographs and the use of his copy of "The Stockyards Hotel" where we found the drawings of N.M. Davidson.

Lucy Hart Knox for photographs.

Marietta Barlow for photographs.

Sidney Jenkins for the use of several photographs.

The people who built my Apple computer and wrote the Applewriter program. Without them this book would still be in my head instead of on paper.

Preface

This is a book about events and the people who did them on the Fort Worth Stockyards. Now that the Fort Worth Stockyards has been saved from the wrecking ball and is a tourist attraction, it is time to tell of some of the things that happened in the area. The things I tell about in this book, I saw or heard or was involved in. There is nothing sensational to read in this book. Since I am not a writer or storyteller, I can only tell what I saw, but in some instances the truth is certainly stranger than fiction.

The Fort Worth Stockyards was a big operation in its day. At any one time there were probably four hundred men on the Yards (including the cattle Yards, hog and sheep Yards, and horse and mule barns) and fifty or sixty men and women in the offices. Very little publicity has been given this group and it is time they were recognized. The great majority of them do not want any recognition and would hide from it if it appeared.

My wife, June, urged me to write this book because I complained a lot about the lack of a book about the Yards and the little recognition given to those who deserved it. So, here it is, the way I saw it. Someone else may have seen it differently — they can write their own book.

Cattle being driven to the scales. Photo courtesy Sid Jenkins.

Sorting "in and by". Photo courtesy Sid Jenkins.

x

Introduction

Why the title "In and By"? One of the major items of work in handling cattle on the Yards was sorting. Cattle were sorted by size, shape, color, weight, sex, age, and any other criteria that could be thought of. There were two accepted ways of sorting. If only two or three cattle needed to be moved out of one pen full to another, the sorters went in the pen, located the cattle they wanted, and with careful handling cut them out of the pen and into the alley. When several pens of cattle needed to be sorted they were sorted in an alley, either "in" (into a pen) or "by" (down the alley). Some were sorted "in" and others "by" and the result was a good load of cattle. I hope that in sorting my recollections "in" and "by" I have "shaped up" an interesting book.

After being exposed to the Fort Worth Stockyards most of my life and having spent ten years there, I saw and learned a lot. I think I am qualified to relate some of the things that I saw, heard, and was involved in. This book is about the cattle Yards only. The sheep and hog Yards operated in a similar manner, but there was a great difference in the way that the animals themselves were handled. In my years on the Yards I never went to the sheep and hog Yards more than a couple of times.

I'm not the one to be writing a book. My qualifications are a couple of years of journalism in high school. I took journalism because it was easier than English, and I was fortunate enough to have gasoline, it being war-time, so I was appointed to drive to the printer's to proofread the high school paper every week. If I took enough time I could miss another class or two.

My father, Clarence Sloan, started to work on the Yards in 1906 or 1907 and spent most of his life there until he died in 1967. He told me lots of tales of the early days on the Yards, but at the time I did not have enough interest in history to remember or appreciate most of them.

Most books and articles on the Yards leave a lot untold and only mention a very few names. There is a simple explanation for this: the stockyards' people were a closemouthed bunch and didn't believe in talking about themselves or their accomplishments, but it's time that recognition was given to that group and time to let it be known that the Yards was a pretty big operation. There was more than one commission company and more than one cattle dealer, and neither could operate without the other. It took a lot of men and a lot of teamwork to make it function.

In the dedication of this book there are names of more than four hundred men and women I personally knew and worked with, and there were another hundred or so whose names I never knew. I don't think I was ever formally introduced to more than five or six of these people. . .you just automatically knew them.

Most authors want to sensationalize the events that happened around the Yards so that it sounds like there was a gunfight every day and a trainload of cattle stolen every night. There were some cattle stolen and a few killings on Exchange Avenue, but the killings were in no way related to cattle trades or cattle rustling on the Yards except that the killer or victim may have worked there.

The ten years that I was there covered the best of times and the worst of times, the time during World War II when meat was a scarce commodity, through the boom of the postwar years, to the senile period of the Yards when it was on its deathbed. Fortunately, I left before it died. I must admit that I couldn't stand to go to the Yards for several years after I left because of the old memories. . .the blood, sweat and tears, the ice, snow, dust, heat, noise, friends, hard times and good times. Even while I write this, it is hard to keep from getting a little misty eyed. In talking to some of the old hands I find that I am not alone in this feeling. It's quite a sensation to go through the building where you spent so many years and see it converted into something you never dreamed you would see, and to see it full of people who would not have set foot in it while it was in its glory.

I can accept some of those changes, but the one that I think is the funniest thing ever is the "Valet Parking Only" sign in front of the Stockyards Hotel.

I can remember the people and events of forty years ago more vividly than those of a few weeks ago. I don't claim to be a writer, but if I don't tell of the things I saw and was part of, I doubt that anyone else will. A few years ago I was talking to an old hand from the Yards and mentioned that I would like to talk to some of the old-timers. It hit home when he said "start talking because we are the old-timers now." I doubt that I contributed to the history of the Yards, but I sure saw a lot of it happen. I am proud of and consider it an honor to have been part of that era on the Yards.

Dedication

This book is dedicated first to my father, Clarence Sloan, who among others was a major part of the history of the Fort Worth Stockyards, who taught me a respect for history, tradition, honesty, integrity, and honor.

Secondly, it is dedicated to the following list of more than four hundred men I personally knew and worked with, the women who worked in the offices and the many others whose names have slipped my memory. I have mentioned some of the women's names, but there were a lot whose names I never knew. Their work was as important as the Yard work; they were a part of the same team.

Some of these people worked a few weeks, others spent their entire lives there. Some of them were worth lots of money, others made and lost fortunes, some became winos and drank themselves to death, some went to prison, some to politics. Some had been involved in killings, others taught Sunday School.

Some were members of exclusive country clubs and some were bounced from "Swede" Burkett's Idle-Hour Club on West Exchange. A few were pompous and overbearing, others were somewhat meek and mild-mannered. Some were extremely outgoing and friendly with everybody, while others were barely tolerated.

If this diverse group of men had one thing in common, it must have been their almost uncanny memory. Any good trader has to remember all the details of his trades to stay in business. But nearly any of these men could recall the weight, cost, quality, and condition of cattle they had bought or sold several years past. C. Sloan could give detailed directions to a ranch that he hadn't been to in thirty years. I talked to several men recently who gave me details of their first day on the Yards over sixty years ago.

The most credit for this book must go to my wife, June Perner Sloan, whose quiet but strong encouragement inspired me to put it together.

Francis Adams	Jeff Albin	Wiley Alliston
James Adams	Afton Allen	Billy Almenrode
Smokey Adams	Boog Allen	Corky Almenrode
Bill Addieway	Emmett Allen	George Almenrode
Herbert Albin	Gary Allen	Dot Alston

Jesse Alvarado
Homer Andrew
Oliver Ball
W.C. Ball
Peanuts Balthrop
Marietta Barlow
Milton Barnes
Ed Barnett
Bill Barse
Roy Barton, Jr.
Gus Bates
Guy Baugh
Clyde Bell
Henry Bell
Jake Bell
J.R. Bettis
H.T. Bibb
John Birdsong
Dr. S.G. Bittick
Dudley Blaine
B.T. Bledsoe
Clifton Bobo
Ernest Bobo
J.P. Bobo
John Bobo
Leroy Bobo
Jim Boorman
Jack Bourland
Frank Bradley
Oscar Brady
Bob Bramlett
Judy Bratcher
Charley Breedlove
Ferris Brock
George Brock
Jack Bullard
Opal Bullard
Raymond Bullard
Bobby Burnett
Buddy Burns
Johnny Burson
Kenneth Burson
Faris Callan

C.M. Callaway
Norman Campbell
Paul Campbell
O.O. Cannon
Wayne Cannon
Bob Cantrell
Red Cardwell
Lee Carrell
Benny Carson
Bobby Carson
Charles Carson
Frank Carson
Shorty Carson
Hub Carter
Jerry Carter
Marcus Carter
Bob Caver
Bob Chandler
Clarence Chappel
L.C. Cheek
Dean Chester
Frances Chester
Wade Choate
Winfred Christian
Wesley Cleveland
Hollis Coggins
Monty Colburn
Ab Cooper
Mel Cooper
Goldie Corbin
Jake Corbin
Jim Corley
Glen Cox
Olen Cox
George Crowley
Charley Daggett
Sheriff Dagley
Gus Davidson
Bruce Davis
Ed Davis
Andy Demolade
Goober Dickson
Hetty Lola Dobkins

Opal Dobkins
A.G. Donovan
Delores Dunlap
R.K. Dunlap
R.K. Dunlap, Jr.
Buck Eubanks
Al Farmer
Carrell Farmer
Max Farmer
J.D. Farmer, Jr.
J.D. Farmer III
Nell Farrell
Son Farrell
Spec Fenner
Bill Few
Homer Fewell
Louis Fields
Harry Fifer
Jim Fisk
Joe Fisk
Ruskin Fisk
Charley Fitzpatrick
Jim Fitzpatrick
Joe Flenniken
Weldon Flenniken
Guy Foley
Sid Foley
Hildegarde Ford
N.G. Fort
Bill Fortenberry
Guinea Fulkerson
Tom Fulps
Porter Funkhouser
Bill Gardenhire
Pie Joe Garrett
Dutch Gause
Joe Gause
Shorty Gause
Speck Gause
T.J. Gause
Earl Gilley
John Good
Rosemary Gouldy

Ted Gouldy
Frank Graves
Sam Graves
Walter Graves
Slim Hagood
Bobby Hamm
Carl Hamm
Paul Hamm
T.Z. Hamm
Cotton Hampton
Darel Hampton
Darel Hampton, Jr.
Tommy Hard
Watt Hardin
Guy Harrell
Harold Harrison
Patsy Harrison
Roy Harrison
Lucy Hart
Tom Hart
Paul Healy
Nubbin Hector
Bill Helm
Will Helm
Boyd High
Clyde Hightower
Davis Hines
Darrell Hirsch
Charlie Hodges
Inge Holland
Tiger Hosea
Lee Holley
Henry Howell
Tom Howell
Jack Huffman
Paul Huffman
Sam Hunnicutt
Houston Hutchens
Bud Jackson
Parker Jameson
Red Jaquess
Lloyd Jary
Lloyd Jary, Jr.

Roland Jary
Bill Jenkins
Dub Jenkins
Sidney Jenkins
Henry Jinkins
Corbie Johnson
Henry Johnson
Joe Johnson
Bill Joyce
Alonzo Keen
C.L. Keen
Clarence Keen
Herman Kennedy
Dewitt Kerr
Edgar Kerr
Herbert Kilgore
Johnnie Kimzie
Marge King
B.M. Kirli
F.E. Kirli
Elmo Klingenberg
Louis Kubitz
Bonnie Kutch
Clyde Kutch
Hilton Kutch
Jeff Kutch
Lester Kutch
Will Lake
Joe Lane
Charlie Laue
Edgar Lee
W.R. Lee
John Lewis
Ward Lindsey
Grady Lisby
Ivy Little
Wade Little
Buck Lovelace
Ben Lotspeich
Al Lowry
Al Lowry, Jr.
Alec Lynch
Alec Lynch, Jr.

H.M. Mack
Doodle Markum
Claude Marrett
Bill Martin
Bill Matthews
Jack Matthews
Shirley Mayhew
Vic Mayhew
Lloyd McBee
Ronnie McBee
Dudley McBride
Charlie McCafferty
Lona McCampbell
O.B. McCampbell
Spec McCarron
L.T. McCoy
Charlie McDaniel
Bob McGaha
Speck McLaughlin
Bob Minton
Herb Minton
Jeff Minton
Jim Mitchell
Louise Mitchell
Cowboy Monroe
Walter Moore
Dick Morgan
John Morris
Sterling Morris
Ted Morris
Roger Muncy
Billy Murray
George Murray
Leo Murray
Connie Myers
Joe Myers
Ed Nelson
Gilbert Nelson
Ben Newby
Edsel Newsom
Peewee Nix
Bob Noble
Bob Noble, Jr.

T.A. Nored
Bert O'Connell
Bob Overton
Mod Overton
Lon Ozee
Doc Parmlee
Val Peacock
Jimmy Penix
J.W. Perryman
Bill Peters
Bill Pier
Weaver Pittman
Van Plankey
Ellis Plaxco
Johnny Plowman
Dallas Pope
Ernest Pope
Fred Porterfield
Charley Poynor
Bill Pugh
Arthur Pulliam
Phil Quinlivan
Frank Quirk
Lou Quirk
John Quirk
Jerry Ralls
Leon Ralls
Lightning Ralls
Henry Ratton
John Ratton
Bob Read
Dan Read
Anson Reese
George Reese
Manson Reese
Murrel Reese
Carl Reppeto
Joe Reppeto
Walter Rice
Charlie Richenstine
Bill Roach
Harvey Roach
Jones Robinson

Wayne Robinson
Joe Rock
Cleve Rodgers
Sam Rodgers
Harry Rosenthal
Wad Ross
Cowboy Roundtree
George Russey
Shorty Russey
Pud Russey
Don Ryan
Pleas Ryan
Fred Ryon
Windy Ryon
Windy Ryon, Jr.
T.B. Saunders
Sonny Saye
George Scaling
Bud Scheets
Charlie Scheets
Wayne Scheets
Johnny Schwartz
Barney Seat
Lute Sensibaugh
Orville Sensibaugh
Johnny Shell
Ray Shelton
George Sheppard
Nina Shepplewich
Darolene Shield
R.B. Shield
Ben Shirley
Ben Shirley, Jr.
Clint Shirley
Denny Simmons
John Simpson
Short Singleton
Happy Skaggs
Corky Sliger
W.O. Sliger
Clarence Sloan
Lanita Smith
Soapy Smith

Gus Stallons
Dan Starnes
Hecky Stetler
Jim Stevenson
Charles Stewart
Wayne Stewart
Billy Straw
Herbert Straw
Pinky Straw
Anna Stubbs
Johnny Stubbs
Jim Sudduth
Ernest Swanzy
Albert Tadlock
Bob Tadlock
Charles Tadlock
Hardy Tadlock
Hardy Tadlock, Jr.
Howard Tadlock
J.A. Tadlock
J.D. Tadlock
Paul Tallas
Charles Team
Bubba Thomason
Charley Thomason
Sam Thomason
Allen Thompson
Bob Thompson
Carnell Thompson
M.Z. Thompson
Otis Thornton
Jeff Tidwell
Jewell Kleinecke Tinsley
Ernest Tuttle
Jim Tuttle
"Little" Jim Tuttle
Dallas Vann
J.D. Vann
John Vick
Elmer "Dutch" Voelkel
Eddie Voelkel
Johnny Walker
Pete Wallace

Jimmie Walsh
Mike Walters
Mike Ward
Al Weaver
Al Weaver, Jr.
Ed Weaver
J.C. Weaver
John Henry Weaver
Phil Weaver
Boots Webb
Burt Weeman
Roy Weeman
Buck Welch
Bill Wells
Walter Wesson

Bob Whatley
Joe Whatley
Edward Whisnant
Maurice Whiteside
Annie Wiggs
George Wilderspin
George Willoughby
Pete Wilshire
Chunky Winnett
Cletes Winnett
Gilbert Winnett
Horace Winnett
Charley Woods
J.P. Woods
Willie Woods

Joe Woody
Loyal Woody
Gib Wright
Harrel Wright
Kelly Wright
Marvin Wright
Bill Yeary
Kathryn Yeary
Burch Young
J.B. Young
Jim Young
Roy Young
Toughy Young
Paul "Red" Yount
Pete Yount.

[1]

My Introduction to the Yards

My first job on the Yards was in the summer of 1935. I was nine years old and was working for Claude "Doc" Minter, who was the manager of the O.M. Franklin Blackleg Serum Company in the Exchange Building. My work consisted of helping Mister Minter fill orders for serum, vaccine and other supplies from the warehouse in a garage behind the building, packing the orders and taking them to the mailbox in the lobby, learning terms like hemorrhagic septicemia and clostridium chauvei septicus bactrin, and drinking soda pop. I think my pay was a dollar a week and all the soda pop I could drink. But as older readers will remember, all you were allowed to drink amounted to no more than two a day. I spent several weeks with him that summer and intended to work for him the next year, but 1936 was the year I got involved with Paul Whiteman and that's another story.

The next time I worked on the Yards was in the summer of 1942, when I worked as a yard hand for my father, Clarence Sloan, who owned and operated Sloan Cattle Company, at that time the largest order-buying operation on the Yards.

Clarence Sloan was an excellent judge of cattle, as were most experienced traders and salesmen, and had a large number of customers in the East. A person had to have an excellent reputation and be a good judge of cattle to survive in the business. The only kind of cattle deals that were ever written down were contracts to buy cattle for future delivery, and not all of them were written. If a buyer said "I'll give so much" for one head, a carload, or

1

GENERAL OFFICE OF LIVESTOCK HOTEL.
OVER $90,000,000.⁰⁰ WAS PAID TO THE
SHIPPERS OF THE SOUTHWEST FOR
LIVESTOCK SOLD ON THIS MARKET
IN 1938.

Drawing of Livestock Exchange Building by N.M. Davidson

a trainload of cattle, he was honor bound to pay for them regardless of the consequences. The same applied if he were selling: he was honor bound to complete the deal. If a person ever backed out on a deal he might as well leave the country because he was finished locally, and his bad reputation would follow him wherever he went.

After graduating from high school in 1944, I went to work on the Yards full time in early 1945. Except for being exposed to A&M in the fall of '45 I was there practically every day until 1955.

My first salary in 1935 was about a dollar a week, as I mentioned. In 1944 and '45 I was getting $25 a week which netted $21.65 after withholding. In 1947 I was making $40 a week and in 1950 or so I got $50. This was pretty much the standard wage at the time for yard hands. Order buyers and salesmen made from $75 or so in the early forties to $100 to $125 by the early fifties.

The four hundred-plus people I mentioned in the dedication of this book covered the human spectrum. There was no seniority or chain of command among the commission companies or order buyers; the lowest paid hand worked with the highest paid ones and might have dealt directly with the richest rancher in the country when the rancher came to the Yards. In other words, the boss could be just as dirty and work just as hard as the flunky.

There was no "bad blood" on the Yards. There were a few men who did not particularly like each other, but they conducted business with each other just the same. If there had been feuds or bad blood, the Yards could not have functioned. True, there were problems that arose from time to time, and if the problem concerned a cattle deal, sometimes a third party was asked to arbitrate. This happened to me once when a salesman weighed me a cripple that I had overlooked. When I could get no satisfaction from the salesman I asked Joe Lane to settle it for me, which he did immediately, in my favor. This was a situation where honor was concerned, but in a gray area. A man was not supposed to weigh to another man any animal that was crippled or in any way unmerchantable. (Try saying that word real fast.) However, a buyer was supposed to be alert and not buy a crip.

[2]

Clarence Sloan,
Cattle Buyer

Clarence Sloan was known to most people as C. Sloan because he didn't like the name Clarence. Strangely enough, there were at least three other men named Clarence on the Yards.

Sloan was born in Cherryvale, Kansas, in July of 1888. The reason I don't give a day is that no one was ever sure of his birthday because he would never give the same date twice. To my knowledge he never posed for more than three photographs and two of these were snapshots. I don't know the reason for his being camera-shy but he was a master at dodging cameras. One of the rare photographs of him is included in this book. It was taken in 1937 when Paul Whiteman, the bandleader, bought a load of cattle for Swift and Company as a publicity stunt.

His father and grandfather were doctors in Missouri and Kansas, and later his father moved to Grayson County, Texas, where his maternal grandparents lived. His maternal grandfather, Harrison Davis, was a prominent farmer and mule raiser in Grayson County. Sloan graduated from Carlisle Military Academy (now University of Texas, Arlington) and attended Texas Agricultural and Mechanical College where he studied engineering.

By 1907 he was on the Yards and in 1911 was working for R.M. Tadlock as a bull buyer. Shortly after this, he married Frances Van Zandt, daughter of Major K.M. Van Zandt, and started trading cattle on his own.

After serving in France and Germany during World War I, he and Roy Vanham formed Vanham Sloan Cattle Company, a clearinghouse, in the twenties. They were doing well financially but lost everything when the Depression hit the Yards in 1929. Many years later Sloan pointed out to me several prominent traders as men who still owed him money from 1929, but to my knowledge few of them ever fully paid their debts.

During this partnership Sloan was trading cattle as well as operating the Vanham Sloan clearinghouse. Sloan also leased the Hick's Ranch north of Saginaw for several years in the twenties. Much of this ranch was later covered by Eagle Mountain Lake. Some of the hands who cowboyed for Sloan on this ranch were Roy Matthews, Sam Stuart, Buck Stuart, Charlie McDaniel, Pony Starr and others. Roy and Sam both became prominent rodeo contestants.

After losing his money in 1929, Sloan was hired by a Fort Worth bank to repossess the Lake Ranch at Pecos. The bank had made a loan on this ranch and had tried several times to repossess it but the party in charge threatened to shoot anyone who tried to evict him. This didn't bother Sloan, who armed himself and did take possession and settle the affair although the other party still blustered that he would kill him on sight. This episode added to Sloan's reputation of not backing away from anyone.

As was the case with most people in the cattle business, Sloan did not let a little thing like being broke stop him. By 1932 he was on the way back in the cattle business. He made some contacts with cattle dealers in Ohio and Virginia that proved profitable over the next fifteen years. In the early thirties he bought lots of cattle in Mexico and shipped them to customers in the East. Later, handling a better class of cattle, he limited his buying area to West Texas.

By 1937 he shipped more than five hundred carloads (about seventeen thousand head) of cattle per year and soon after was the biggest operator on the Yards, a position he held for several more years. By 1950, having populated Virginia, Ohio, Kentucky, West Virginia, Tennessee, Alabama, Georgia, Maryland and Pennsylvania with cattle, he semi-retired. Although Sloan was financially well off, the fear of losing his money again never allowed him to enjoy it. Like all the old-timers at the Yards, he felt the place couldn't open without him, so he continued going to the Yards almost daily until his death in April 1967.

Sloan was small in size, only about five foot seven. He was dark-complected and usually a very quiet man. He did not socialize much in later years, but I hear he did a lot of it in his bachelorhood when he lived at the Fort Worth Club. Sloan was a neat dresser, even to polished shoes (I never saw him wear a pair of shoes more than three or four times between polishings). As soon as an article of clothing showed a little wear, he got rid of it. He was polite to the ladies, always standing and removing his hat when he talked to them.

He was a master at giving me what is now known as a "guilt trip." Many times I would be dressed and ready to leave the house on a date, when he would mention that it looked like snow and his poor steers might freeze to death before morning. So I would change clothes, saddle a horse, pen the cattle in the barn, change clothes again and arrive for my date an hour or so later than planned.

There was only one person in the world who could con Sloan into anything and that was a hand who worked for him for several years. This hand could talk Sloan into financing horses or cars for him, lending him money that he was not thinking of paying back and many other schemes. Two or three of Sloan's hands threatened to quit if he didn't fire this man, but Sloan talked them out of the notion and kept him for another year or so.

There was a rancher in southern Wise County who was known as a hard trader and was difficult to deal with. This man had good quality cattle that were wanted by many traders, but because of the rancher's disposition not too many of them tried to deal with him. Sloan often told that one day a fancy dressed city-type man wearing spats and a derby hat drove his buggy (this was in the early days) to the man's ranch and said he wanted to buy some cattle. The rancher thought he would make a killing on someone dressed like this buyer, so he showed him his herd. The buyer seemed to notice only the sorriest cattle in the herd and commented on what "beautiful animals" they were. The rancher knew he "had it made" and sold his herd to the city-slicker, allowing him to sort the cattle as he saw fit. The cattle were to be delivered the next week. When the buyer arrived to sort and receive the cattle he was dressed in the working clothes of a cowman and proceeded to cut out all the "beautiful animals" he had described the week before and take only the best of the herd. The rancher was the one taken on the deal and the buyer came out in good shape. Sloan would never tell who the buyer was, but I have enough evidence to know that it was Sloan himself.

Clarence Sloan was not the first or last cattle dealer on the Yards, but for a few years he was the biggest, and did his share in adding to the history of the Yards.

[3]

The Day-to-Day Routine

Let me take you through a few typical days on the Yards as it was in my time. It was not much different in the earlier days and was still basically the same until the auction sale became the major activity at the Yards.

In the thirties and earlier, the Yards were operating six days a week. When they got "soft" in the early forties, they started closing on Saturday. Buyers were able to buy cattle anytime there was enough daylight to see the cattle.

Buyers and traders met in the lobby of the Exchange Building every morning at six or so, depending on the time of year, and "matched" to determine the order in which they could look at cattle at the commission companies. To allow buyers a "turn" at a commission company and to prevent favoritism to a buyer, matching was necessary because there may have been several buyers for one class of cattle and only one or two commission companies might have this class for sale. This was not necessarily the best way to determine this, but no one ever came up with a better idea.

When the matching began each morning, the order buyers or someone representing them sat in a circle on the west side of the lobby using Coke cases (they were wooden in those days) for seats. For most of my time at the Yards, Ernest "Inky" Bobo was the dealer. He used a deck of cards that included the spades and enough other cards to allow one card for each buyer in the circle. After shuffling the cards he proceeded clockwise around the circle to turn up a card for each man. If the card was a spade,

CHAMBER MAIDS
ROOMS ARE KEPT CLEAN AND SANITARY.
ALL ARE DISINFECTED FREQUENTLY TO
PREVENT ANY CHANCE OF INFECTION.

Cleaning pens, an all too familiar scene
N.M. Davidson drawing

he called out the number and the name of the buyer; if not a
spade, the buyer got nothing. If the ace of spades was turned up,
the buyer got a first with the commission company being matched
for at that time, a deuce of spades meant a second, etc. After the
circle had been called, the cards were reshuffled, the caller moved
on to the next commission company on the list, and the process
was repeated until thirteen rounds (the number of companies and
groups of companies) had been completed. When a buyer bought
cattle from the commission company the salesman gave his weigher the buyer's name, selling price, and how the cattle were to be
weighed. The weigher had already made a list of owners and pen
numbers; now he had a list of buyers to go with it. Many buyers
and salesmen got their experience from years spent working as
a weigher. The commission companies also had a form of matching to see who could weigh first, and they usually weighed for a
hour at a time during heavy runs of cattle. Sometimes the commission companies weighed only one or two drafts during their
turn. During lighter runs it was first come first served at the scales.

The weighers sometimes used a card listing all the transactions,
but the best of them kept hundreds of transactions in their heads
with nothing on paper. Charley Thomason started to work for
Johnny Schwartz as a weigher many years ago. To impress
Schwartz with his ability and thoroughness he made out a card

with all shippers, cattle and pen numbers. He showed the card to Schwartz, who looked the card over, told Charley it looked good, then tore it up and told him to keep all the information in his head.

At one time a couple of the faster weighers were Dub Jenkins and Nubbin Hector, who worked for National Livestock Commission Company. Once they had a dispute with the commission company over pay and did not show up for work the next time there was a big run. It was pretty funny to see people from the sheep Yards as well as some of the office staff trying to sort out the cattle and get them weighed. Needless to say, they all worked pretty late that night and Jenkins and Hector were welcomed back. This was one of the few incidents that resembled a strike among the yard hands, but the Stockyards Company hands did have a couple of strikes while I was there. There was no violence or anything sensational about the strikes and I think the union got whatever it was demanding. These strikes were called during light runs and only lasted a couple of days.

Some of the other top weighers during my time were Bill Gardenhire, Bill Addieway, Charley Thomason, Herb Kilgore, Sidney Jenkins, and Wade Choate. These were only a few of them. Most of them went on to be top salesmen and buyers and some of them eventually owned commission companies. Hector later joined the Border Patrol for a year or so, then returned to the Corner where he died from a beating. "yard hands" worked for commission companies, order buyers and speculators. Their duties consisted of taking care of cattle, feeding, driving, sorting, etc., and also included cleaning pens. I could have said something besides "cleaning pens" and it would have been perfectly acceptable in this day and time. Although a lot of the people on the Yards were as tough as could be and their language was as foul and dirty as anywhere in the world, there was an unwritten law that language was kept clean around women and this was pretty well the way it was with very few exceptions.

Jewell Tinsley told me that in the many years she worked in the Building there was never a time that she was not treated like a lady, which, of course, she was. There were very few who were not in that category. When a woman visited the Yards, her presence was known and passed on to anyone close by so that language was proper and clean in most cases, but there were certainly exceptions.

The Stockyards Company men, being union men, were able to keep reasonably regular hours sometimes with overtime, but the other hands including buyers and commissionmen had no idea of what regular hours were. A typical day started at five or six in the morning and could end as early as eight or nine a.m. or as late as eight or nine p.m. I remember once when I didn't get home until two a.m. and barely had time to bathe and eat so I could be back at the Yards by five a.m. I knew some people who didn't even go home for two or three days at a stretch.

You might think that a person working in such an environment might not pay much attention to cleanliness, but ninety-nine percent showed up clean and smelling good every morning. There were a couple of exceptions, though, who usually bathed a couple of times a month, whether they needed to or not.

After a long hot day you could get pretty dirty. Since we had no facilities for cleaning up (no OSHA) we often used a water trough for a bathtub, but only in the summer. After this bath you were clean enough to go home and get a real bath. It could be exciting when one of your friends got a bucket of ice water out of the cooler and poured it on you in the "tub." We were lucky for a while; one of the boys found an unlocked door in the building where Billy Bob's Texas is now located, and discovered running water in the showers. We were a pretty clean bunch until somebody with the City of Fort Worth locked the door a few weeks later.

If you were a yard hand, your day started around six a.m. or whenever it was light enough to see and your pens had been unlocked by the keyman. You had to clean and fill the water troughs, put fresh hay in the hay mangers, feed cottonseed hulls if necessary and order whatever amount of feed that might be needed to start the day. Multiply this by the number of pens you had (seven, in our case) and it could take a while to complete the job. Then you could have a few minutes off. In most cases, you did not have every pen full of cattle in the mornings because traders tried to get all their cattle shipped out before going home the previous day, but you had to put feed in the empty pens for the cattle that would be bought during the day.

Company	Place	Places
Crow	0	Goldie, Albin — Cheek, HV
K.T.	10	Weaver, Fort — Inge, R
Clay	7	Roach, Albin — B.Weaver, Jack Bullard
Tex	4	R, HV — Jf. Gause
No.T.	3	R, Raymond Bullard — Roach
Day.	0	Albin, Roach — Graves, Fat
Cass.	11	Goldie, Graves — Blaine, Jf.Gause
For.W.K.	4	Blaine, Cheek — R
Nored	4	Goldie, Roach — Albin
Ralls	10	HV, Albin — Inge, Fort
Jary	2	R.Bullard — Graves, Blaine
Fifer	6	Roach, Albin — Fort, Goldie
Ship/Bal.	8	Cheek, Graves — R.Bull, Goldie

Matching card. Left column lists commission companies, center is place, third shows first four places. In fourth row, Sloan had a fourth at Texas behind Rodgers & Lane, Hampton-Voelkel, and Jeff Gause.

If you worked for a man who might have a pasture within ten or twelve miles of the Yards, you might have to go to the pasture to feed cattle there, then return to the Yards.

After feeding, depending on the time of day, you might be expected to clean the pens or alleys. The Stockyards Company had a crew that cleaned the pens and alleys, but they only had two tractors with loaders, six or eight trucks and twelve or fourteen men to clean the whole Yards. In most cases they could handle the job, but if they ever got behind for any reason it took a long time to catch up. When the Stockyards Company could not get to your pens and alleys (main alleys had priority over pens) you had to clean them yourself and pile manure in the alleys.

If you never saw the Yards when it needed cleaning, there's no way to accurately describe it. Twelve or more inches of manure mixed with straw and compacted by hundreds of hooves has the consistency of adobe when it is damp and the adhesiveness of hot asphalt when it is thoroughly wet. You could get a real thrill when walking through it to have it pull your boots off. Even though most of the Yards was paved with brick, there were some sections of alleys and a few pens that had no bricks on them. These were used mostly to keep sore-footed cattle or as a place to ride a young horse that might buck you off. There was a dirt alley by number two scale and I never did understand its purpose, but it held a lot of water when it rained and we had to detour by another route in wet weather.

After a buyer had bought several cattle and notified you of his buys, you started out to pick up the cattle. You planned your pickup depending on the location of the scales where your cattle would be weighed. If there were only a few to be picked up at number five (the farthest away) and you knew that they would be weighed late, you might start at number one or number two (closer) and work your way back to your division. I might add that you nearly always planned a stop for a cup of coffee in the Building if there was time. Before Windy Ryon started his western store in the lobby of the Building, you might sit around the lobby on Coke cases from Charlie Richenstine's Coke stand, or go out on the porch and sit around to kill time when you had to wait an hour or so for some of your cattle to be weighed. The hardest work on the Yards was the waiting. I didn't mind the work, but the waiting was murder, especially if you had nearly everything done for the day and had to wait a couple of hours for two or three head to be weighed at some far-off place like number five.

Sometimes we had a lot of time to visit on the Yards. If you had any length of time (sometimes an hour or so) to wait at a scale for your cattle, you could go to the Building or sit around the scale house or the commission company booth and visit with others who had to wait, too. Sometimes there might be as many as twelve or fifteen hands waiting to pick up.

Lots of people nowadays have antique brass spittoons in their homes for decorations. If those people had seen the hundreds of spittoons in the Building in actual use they sure wouldn't want them in their home. It's about to gag me just remembering them as I write this. No way could I stand to pick one up even if it had been sterilized in a hospital.

A popular pastime or bad habit, depending on how you look at it, was whittling. About half of the men on the Yards whittled, but I don't remember of anyone during my time whittling anything useful. Anytime a group sat around, whether talking business or shooting the bull, pocketknives appeared and the whittling started.

Anything made of wood was fair game for the whittler. It made no difference if it was a supporting post for a booth, the bench they were sitting on, a fence, feed trough, or even woodwork or furniture in the Exchange Building, it was whittled, and quite a few items were ruined by the whittlers. Not all whittling was intentional, some whittlers just had the habit and unconsciously opened up a knife and went to work on any available wood. To prevent whittling, which really was destructive to necessary items, a tin edging was nailed around most things that could be damaged such as water coolers, benches, booth posts, etc.

All the fenceposts on the Yards were fine quality northern cedar, soft, straight-grained, and perfect for whittling. Anytime an old post was removed from a fence, it gathered a group of whittlers and was cut into handy-size pieces faster than a bunch of buzzards could clean up a rabbit. If several whittlers were sitting around with some good cedar, the shavings could literally cover the ground around them. I might add that all knives were kept as sharp as possible and you could shave with most of them.

After making the rounds of the scales, signing for cattle and copying weights from scale tickets, chasing down a calf or two that may have turned back on you, and bringing the cattle to your division, you either started on another pickup or began sorting cattle.

In very few cases were cattle shipped to the customer as they had been bought from the commission company. There were always some too large or too small for the load you were working on, and they were sorted out to go in another load.

Cattle were driven to the end of an alley, then driven one by one down the side of the alley by the man doing the sorting and sometimes one or more yard hands depending on the length of the alley. As they were cut from the bunch, the sorter called out "in" or "by" to the man working the gate into the pen. If "in" was called, the gate was opened and the animal turned in; if "by" was called, the animal was driven on by the gate and held at the other end of the alley until the sort was completed. The cycle was repeated over and over until all the cattle were sorted by color, size, shape, sex, quality, etc., according to the way they were to be shipped. If a lot of sorting was necessary, pens on both sides of the alley might be used. This worked so long as the sorter remembered which pen was for which animals.

This job sounds like it takes only a few minutes, but if you were sorting a hundred or so animals into five or six different classes, you had to repeat the operation over and over. If any cattle got by the gate man, then you had to go into the pen and get out the mistakes. Once a load was sorted, you checked them carefully to see if they were all the same size and shape and looked good together. If not, sort again.

After sorting, the cattle were fed. Later in the day when you had the load complete and thought they had gained enough weight to be profitable, you drove them to number four scale where they were weighed to your customer, turned over to the Stockyards Company and driven to the shipping division. Depending on the season and the number of orders you had, you might ship one load or fifteen or more.

Weight gain meant profit to the trader, but the amount of gain had to be reasonable or it could hurt the trader's reputation. Cattle will lose a lot of weight on a train trip of several days, and if they had had an excessive amount of fill and then showed a lot of shrink on arrival, it could cost the trader a customer. A lot of care was necessary to see that the cattle gained just the right amount of weight and no more.

When cattle were quiet, had a lot of clean hay and a trough full of clean water with a faucet that was gurgling and trickling a small stream, they would put on a lot of weight in a couple of hours. There was an art to making the faucet trickle just right and the drain plug had to be set so that the inflow and outflow of water was balanced. The Stockyards Company frowned on this practice because it wasted a lot of water and stockyards hands were ordered to turn off trickling faucets if they saw them.

C. Sloan estimated that a calf would gain about a dime per swallow. He liked to watch cattle standing at the water trough and count the dimes. Not all fill was profit because the cattle lost some weight in all the handling they went through after leaving the commission company and it took some fill just to break even.

Around noon, you could go get something to eat. If you didn't have a lot to do you could drive some distance from the Yards to eat, but if you were busy the best thing was to grab something in the Building at Charlie's Coke stand, or from one of the vendors who made the rounds of the Yards.

During my time there were no real good eating places close to the Yards. The Cattlemen's restaurant opened, I believe, in 1947, but the prices were a little steep for the ordinary hands who only ate there occasionally. There were several "greasy spoon" type cafes in the area but too much grease doesn't mix with hard work. If someone discovered a new or better place to eat, it wasn't long before a lot of hands were eating there. Some of the popular eating places at the time were The Up-To-Date Cafe, Anne's, Skyline Grill, Dear's Barbecue, Massey's, Herman Grubis', Farmer's, Heinie's, and several others that I can't recall. I remember hearing about the Texas City explosion on the car radio in 1947 when we were on our way to eat at Massey's on Jacksboro Highway. Several of us were among the first customers of Herb Massey's when he opened his restaurant on Eighth Avenue after leaving his brother's restaurant on Jacksboro Highway.

Any time that C. Sloan went with us to eat we always let him pay for the food, so he didn't go with us too often. The main reason, though, was that he wanted to sit around and watch the cattle fill. Sloan complained of a bad stomach for years. I think one of the reasons for the stomach problem was the standing order he gave us to bring him when we went to eat: two pieces of dry bread with a thick piece of American cheese between them and a cup of coffee.

A man known as Shorty made the rounds of the Yards during the cooler months selling homemade tamales. He carried them in a couple of ten-gallon lard cans lined with newspapers. I don't know how he kept them as hot as he did, but they warmed many a stomach on cold winter days. I think he sold them for fifty cents a dozen and we thought he was robbing us. A man named Johnson was on the Yards around noon every day for a couple of years. He sold sandwiches that helped you get by. He supposedly had had a contract to furnish sandwiches for the county jail and we accused him of selling us sandwiches that the prisoners wouldn't eat.

A man from Newark named Slim sold sandwiches, candy, and ice cream. He usually worked from about ten in the morning until four or five or later in the afternoon and worked there for several years. He usually worked around the drive-in gate or the north part of the Yards. Stockyards Company employees could not leave the Yards to eat so they brought their lunches. Quite often they had to eat "on the run" because business didn't stop for anything. Since there were potbellied coal stoves in the scale houses, the Stockyards Company hands always had warm food in the winter.

Just because you had shipped everything didn't mean the day was over. You still had to feed the remaining cattle, drain the water troughs and lock the pens. There was a certain way to lock the pens; if they were not locked properly, the keyman was not supposed to unlock them. Water troughs were drained at night for several reasons. One was that cattle would drink more water if they had had none for several hours. Another reason was that water needed to be kept clean for the cattle, and there was a danger of feed or manure getting in the trough at night.

Before you locked the pens you had to be sure that all the cattle that had been bought had been picked up. When Darel Hampton worked for Clarence Sloan, he was notorious for buying one or two head at the end of the day from Alonzo Keen, who

weighed at number five. I hated to answer the phone fifteen or
twenty minutes after Darel left because I knew the message would
be "I bought a couple from Alonzo and he will weigh 'em in a
little while" or "Lonzo weighed me a couple I bid on this morning." This caused us to make a late trip to number five or number
one to pick up one or two head. After Darel went into business
for himself, Sloan would manage to buy one or two when he was
on his way to the Building at the end of the day.

Most of the traders liked to sit around and talk after the work
was apparently over and many times I begged to leave for the
day so I could get some work done at home, but I was always
told that "if you have a store, you have to keep it open." This
may be true, but I doubt that C. Sloan ever sold over a dozen
head a year this late in the day.

Every Friday, cattle that would be held over the weekend
had to be weighed to make the paperwork balance out. When
the cattle were weighed, the scale ticket was marked "Invoice"
and this ticket was proof that the operator had the correct number
of cattle. In this case, the cattle were not handled by the Stockyards Company but were taken back to the pens by the trader.
If a trader needed to know the weight of a bunch of cattle he
could drive them to the scales and obtain a "catch weight" on
them. Again, they were taken back by the trader.

Not every cattle deal was made by weight. If cattle were sold
by the head instead of weight, they were driven to the scales and
"counted across" to the buyer. In this way, the Stockyards Company recorded the transaction by the number of head.

Some traders, particularly the smaller ones, would sell cattle
for "two bits on the ticket." This meant that they would transfer
the weight of the animal when they bought it to the customer
and charge twenty-five cents per hundred pounds for a profit. The
price could be negotiated, of course. By doing this, the trader was
not concerned about a fill on the animal. I've seen lots of outsiders
bid this way on cattle because they were afraid that the trader
would try to get to them. Cattle that were being transferred were
driven to the scales and "counted across" like sales by the head.
The weighmaster made a transfer ticket showing the weight, number
of head and ticket number of the original scale ticket.

Another chore was making trips to the Building to deliver
scale tickets or other information to the girls in the office or pick

up a clearance for cattle being shipped by truck. After I had been on the Yards a couple of years, I was bonded so that I could sign clearances without having to make the long round trip to the building.

The day had started at six in the morning and it might now be six or seven or later at night. Although there were times when we worked sixteen or eighteen hours or even more, there were a lot of times during the slack winter months that we did not work over two or three hours a day on the Yards. During those times we spent a lot of hours working in the country. Nearly all the buyers and commissionmen ran cattle in the country, and during the off season we usually worked on fixing pens and fences and other chores on their land.

[4]

Wheelers and Dealers

Two entities on the Yards that absolutely could not survive without each other were the dealers and commission companies. Without the dealers, the commission companies would be able to sell only to the packing houses. Without the commission companies, the dealers would have no cattle to buy.

The name "cattle dealer" covers several different types of individuals or companies. There is the order buyer who is bonded to buy cattle only when he has an order for them. The speculator or trader does not have to have an order to buy cattle, but buys them hoping he can resell to an order buyer, packing house or outsider who may be looking for cattle. The terms speculator, order buyer, cattle buyer, trader, cattle dealer, or cattle broker were used rather loosely and could at times apply to nearly anyone on the Yards. At some time or another any cattle buyer had to take some cattle he did not want in order to fill his orders and therefore had some extra cattle to dispose of. He had to try to sell them to another trader or plant them with a commission company and hope to make a profit.

To eliminate a lot of confusion, I will use the term "buyer" to cover all types of traders, dealers, etc. A buyer or company could be one individual or a dozen or more in the business of buying cattle.

If an individual buyer was in business for himself he was the whole crew, from yard hand to boss. An individual might have no more than a couple of pens assigned to him by the Stockyards

20

WEIGHING
CORRECT WEIGHING IS IMPORTANT.
TO INSURE THIS, ALL SCALES ARE CHECKED
AND TESTED FREQUENTLY BY FACTORY
EXPERTS UNDER GOVERNMENT REGULA-
TIONS, SO SELLERS AND BUYERS CAN
FEEL CONFIDENT THAT WEIGHTS
ARE ABSOLUTELY ACCURATE.

Cattle being counted off number one scale. N.M. Davidson drawing.

Company, while a large firm could have a dozen or more pens and maybe three or four buyers and six or eight yard hands.

Although there was a lot of paperwork required, no individual, whether he was a buyer or a small commission man, had enough work to require a full-time secretary or a large office. Most of them had office space and clerical help in a larger office or clearinghouse.

Some buyers owned their own booths while others shared. Sloan, for instance, shared his booth with a couple of other buyers for many years. In most cases this was a free rent proposition with the exception of the telephone bill.

Practically all of the order buyers seemed to take a turn being the biggest operator on the Yards, but none of them held the status longer than a few years and I can't recall any that ever got to the top again after losing it. At one time Clarence Sloan was the biggest operator, having six or eight hands working for him as well as a couple of buyers. He stayed on top during the late thirties and early forties. After he slowed down in 1946, Sloan bought and sold more than thirteen thousand head (almost one million dollar's worth) and his profit was about two dollars per head.

After Sloan lost out, Allen & Flenniken (who later became Rodgers & Lane) held the lead for some time, then lost out to

Thompson, Tuttle & Thompson, who later lost out to J.D. Vann (later Vann-Roach). I am not familiar with too many buyers before C. Sloan, but there were many others. Maybe one reason for the ever-changing lead is that most of these buyers shipped cattle to one or two geographic areas, and after a few years of shipping breeding stock to an area the local people were raising their own cattle and the dealer became a victim of his own success.

Some of the buyers of my time, operating under their own or various company names, were Walter Graves, Dutch Voelkel, Eddie Voelkel, Darel Hampton, Jeff Albin, Herbert Albin, M.Z. Thompson, Bob Thompson, Ernest Tuttle, Sam Rodgers, Boog Allen, Joe Flenniken, J.A. Tadlock, Albert Tadlock, Hardy Tadlock, Peewee Nix, Goldie Corbin, Big Windy Ryon, Hecky Stetler, Mel Cooper, Wiley Alliston, L.C. Cheek, Hilton Kutch, Bob Noble, Dallas Vann, J.D. Vann, Phil Weaver & Sons, Joe Garrett, Dudley Blaine, Jack Bullard, Raymond Bullard, Buddy Burns, Norman Campbell, Paul Campbell, Clarence Chappel, Winfred Christian, Joe Fisk, Ruskin Fisk, N.G. Fort, Roy Harrison, Harrel Wright, Jack Huffman, Paul Huffman, Dewitt Kerr, Wade Little, Ivy Little, Bill Matthews, O.B. McCampbell, George Reese & Son, Harvey Roach, Bill Roach, Wayne Robinson, Orville Sensibaugh, Jim Stevenson, George Wilderspin, and several more. Many of the buyers were, or had been, in partnership with others and a lot of them had been in several different partnerships.

Most buyers specialized in certain types of cattle. For instance, Sloan handled mostly Hereford and Angus stocker steers and heifers. Occasionally he would handle orders for Hereford or Angus cows but hardly ever any plain-type cattle.

One company never got any larger or smaller in the many years that it operated there and that was J. A. Tadlock & Sons. The reason is that the Tadlocks bought only bulls and nothing else. All the yard hands were jealous of the Tadlocks because they always left the Yards several hours before anybody else got through. There was a simple reason for this: the bulls were a nuisance. They were always fighting each other and had to be kept in separate pens at the commission companies. The companies needed to get the bulls weighed and out of their way so that they could have more room. To do this, they weighed every bull to Tadlock as soon as possible. The Tadlocks picked up the bulls early to get them out of the scale pens where they were also causing problems. The Tadlocks sold most of the bulls to the packers by the pen full and as a result their work was over fairly early in the day.

Smaller, individual operators covered the entire Yards alone buying cattle. Some of the larger operators with several buyers assigned their buyers to specific commission companies, similar to the way the packers operated.

A couple of small traders would sit around the Building and when they saw a stranger come in they would corner him and try to get his business. One of these men was a notorious liar who would tell any story to turn business his way, even telling some that the man the stranger was looking for had died or gone out of business.

Commission companies were in the business of selling cattle for owners who shipped their cattle to Fort Worth. They acted as agents for the owners and showed the cattle in the best way possible to bring the best price. The commission companies sorted cattle so that the best ones would be shown together. One bad animal in a pen can bring the same result as a bad apple in a bushel. Commission companies sent representatives to the country to drum up business for themselves and the Fort Worth Stockyards. Commission companies could not operate if there were no buyers, so everybody had to get along with each other.

The larger commission companies might have a calf salesman, cow salesman, sheep salesman, and hog salesman plus a head yardman, head weigher, driver and two or three other yardmen plus an owner or two and an office staff of six or eight. The smaller ones, just like the dealers, were a one-man operation. Sometimes five or six of these one- or two-man companies would hire an individual to represent all of them as a hog and sheep salesman. Most companies handled all types and breeds of cattle, sheep and hogs. Since I was on the sheep Yards maybe once or twice in my ten-year tour of duty, I won't try to give any details of their operation. None of the commission companies were involved in the horse and mule business but a lot of the horse and mule men had ranches and traded in cattle.

The larger commission companies were National Livestock Commission Company, Daggett-Keen Commission Company, Texas Livestock Marketing Association, and Cassidy Southwestern Commission Company. Slightly smaller were Keen & Sons, John Clay and Company, George W. Saunders, Woody-Kutch, Farmer, Foley-

Allen, Nored-Hutchens, Jerry Ralls, Fifer, Shirley, and Jary Commission Company. Smaller still were Bill Barse, George Crowley, Clyde Kutch, Kahn-Thornton, Carson, Hamm, Breedlove, Drive-In, Helm, Howell Brothers, Hunnicutt, Lone Star, Pete Wallace, Marvin Wright, and Jimmie Walsh. Even though some of the companies were small in size, any of them could have shippers that might send them several loads of cattle at a time. Commissionmen, like order buyers, formed partnerships and changed their company names quite often. In all cases commission companies were referred to by a shortened name: Texas for Texas Livestock Marketing Association, Daggett for Daggett-Keen Commission Company, etc.

Commission companies were also like order buyers in that they seemed to take turns at being the largest. This, of course, was due to their management, ability to provide services and get the best prices for their customers. Some of the largest were locally owned while others were a branch operation of a company that usually had offices in Chicago, Omaha, St. Louis, Denver, Kansas City, Oklahoma City, Houston and San Antonio. The small one- or two-man operations were locally owned.

Several of the commission companies provided an order buying service. In some cases a salesman would double as an order buyer, while some of the larger companies hired men who were full-time order buyers.

Every operator on the Yards had to be bonded, have money to operate, office space, and some pens. In the case of commission companies, some regulations of the Packers and Stockyards Act of 1921 required that certain amounts of money be set aside in certain accounts in order to operate. This was to guarantee that payment could be made immediately to shippers when their cattle were sold. The United States Department of Agriculture didn't like the idea of checks floating or bouncing. Some of the smaller operators simply did not have the capital to finance their operations, so the clearinghouse was the answer.

The largest clearing house operators during my time were T.B. Saunders and Company, and Thornton and Company. Several commission companies, including Foley-Allen, cleared a few traders and dealers.

A clearinghouse operator would furnish operating money, office space and clerical help for a percentage of the money used. I think this rate was also regulated by the Packers and Stockyards Act. Some, but not all, of the larger commission companies acted as a clearinghouse for one, two, or several operators. T.B. Saunders & Company was one of the larger clearinghouses. Tom furnished money and office space for quite a few traders and commission companies. C. Sloan lost a ton of money operating a clearinghouse in 1929, and even when he was the largest operator on the Yards he refused to use his own money, but operated through Tom Saunders. In later years he was offered a private office and a lot of fringe benefits by one of the larger commission companies if he would let them handle his business, but he refused to move.

Most clearinghouses consisted of one large office with a roll-top desk for each commission company. There was a small wooden sign painted green with gold letters on each desk. I don't know if the shape and color of the signs was regulated, but I believe every one in the building was the same type. The operator had his own phone on his desk, and at night he could close and lock the roll top with the phone safely inside.

To communicate rapidly enough to take advantage of market prices, telegrams were used a lot until the late thirties. Letters were not fast enough. Although things were pretty modern in the forties and fifties, not every farm or ranch had a telephone and communications were sometimes difficult between buyers and sellers. In some cases it was necessary to leave messages for customers at the local feed store or filling station. In some small towns it was necessary to go to the local telephone office to make a long distance call. One reason for this was to give the customer a chance to talk in private because most of the rural lines were party lines and most people didn't care to let everybody know their business. In many cases arrangements were made by mail or telegram to expect a phone call on a certain night and time.

I've noticed recent television commercials about the telephone companies switching calls all around the nation electronically, in a few seconds. This is a far cry from the many nights I got a geography lesson listening to the long distance operator call city after city routing a call to a customer in Virginia or Kentucky. If you placed a person-to-person call in those days the operator didn't give up until she located your party. I have heard operators call six or eight stores or houses in a rural town trying to locate the party, sometimes taking an hour to locate him.

Sometime in the early fifties, a privately owned paging system was installed at the Yards. For a monthly fee subscribers could call Thornton's office, where the unit was kept, and have them page someone on the Yards. Several speakers were installed and pretty well covered the Yards. The service was used by a lot of people but C. Sloan was too tight to subscribe.

In most cases, a clearinghouse was a safe investment if the owner was careful in screening the traders he cleared. However, clearing business for a few questionable operators could be pretty risky because it didn't take very many carloads of cattle to run into a lot of dollars. During my time there were a few operators who cost their clearinghouses a lot of money because of shady deals, and in some cases the operator was barred from trading on the Yards by the U.S. Department of Agriculture. In one case, known to most people on the Yards, a trader lost a bunch of money on a cattle deal and the owner of the clearinghouse got his name removed from the trader's bond but left another trader to stand the loss, which was tremendous. Mentioning names in this case won't help anything because the ones who need to know, already do.

[5]

The Stockyards Company

The Fort Worth Stockyards Company did not buy or sell cattle. It provided and maintained the facilities and furnished the labor to transfer ownership of cattle for commission companies and traders. It sold all the feed that was used and no other feed was allowed. If I remember correctly, Stockyards Company personnel were not allowed to trade in cattle.

The men who worked for the Fort Worth Stockyards Company were union members and all had titles such as Weighmaster, Gate Man, Driver, Key Man, Counter, Hay Wagon Driver or Helper, and Carpenter. Each job had rank and seniority. The weighmaster was the man in overall charge of the scales where cattle were weighed. I think weighmaster was the highest ranking position, just under a foreman's rating. The gate man opened and closed the gate onto the scale, and the counter let animals off the scale, counted them and assigned them to catch pens to be picked up by the buyers. Drivers then drove the cattle to the pens assigned to them and locked the gate. There was another class of driver that worked the night shift and delivered cattle from the drive-in gate to the commission companies (this job was handled by the commission company driver during the day). A crew was on duty night and day at the drive-in gate because cattle were shipped and received at all hours.

All Stockyards Company men carried keys, but only a key man could legally unlock a pen of cattle for anyone. All movements of cattle by the Stockyards Company were recorded and

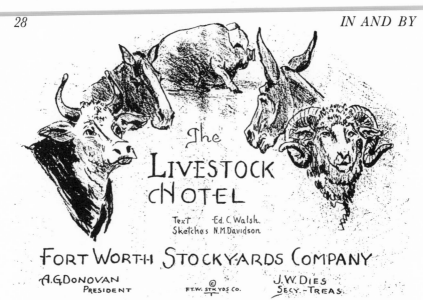

The
LIVESTOCK
cHOTEL

Text   Ed. C. Walsh.
Sketches N.M.Davidson

FORT WORTH STOCKYARDS COMPANY

A.G.DONOVAN   J.W. DIES
PRESIDENT   FT.W. STK YDS CO.   SECY.-TREAS.

Cover of brochure printed by Fort Worth Stockyards Company. N.M. Davidson drawing.

they were very particular about this. When you went to a scale to pick up cattle you started yelling "keyo, keyo, keyo" for the key man as far away as you thought he could hear you. One reason for this was to try to get ahead of somebody else who was on the way to pick up cattle at the same scale, because it was first come first served. If you could beat the other person you could sometimes save as much as twenty or thirty minutes.

The Stockyards Company had a large crew of carpenters under B.D. Webb, who was the foreman for many years. The hay men drove the hay wagons, each pulled by one big Percheron horse, and delivered hay to individual hay racks or fed it to your cattle if you asked for the service.

Not to run down the hay haulers, but they always fed hay from the top of the fences or walkways and if any hay fell on the ground, that's where it stayed. For this reason you asked the hay barn to feed your pens only in an emergency. To order hay and feed you would call the hay barn and talk to Monty Colburn or Dan Starnes and might say: "Rack six bales on (pen number) 30-24, four on 30-28, feed two in 30-41, two bales of alfalfa and three sacks of hulls in the booth." This did not mean to feed the hulls in the booth but to store them there.

The hay wagons were not very big, maybe five feet by eight or ten feet. They had wooden wheels with steel tires and, since they were pulled by one horse, they could be turned around in the alleys. The Stockyards Company tried using trucks to haul hay but there was no way that they could compete with the horse and wagon.

The scale houses were fairly large and were built of bricks stuccoed like the Exchange Building. The weighmaster was in overall charge of everything that took place in or around the scale. It took many years to get a weighmaster's job. Most of the Stockyards Company superintendents and foremen were qualified as weighmasters and took over when necessary. I can't remember the names of all the weighmasters, but some of them were Burch Young, Roy Young, Lee Holley, Charlie McCafferty, Edgar Lee, Bob Caver, and "Sheriff" Dagley. Some of the superintendents and foremen I remember were Johnny and Kenneth Burson, Gilbert Nelson, Ben Newby, Paul Tallas, W.R. Lee, "Mo" Klingenberg, B.M. Kerlee, and B.D. Webb.

The scale house was home to its crew of at least six (weighmaster, counter, gate man, key man, two or more drivers). There was a large room in the center that held a large coal-burning stove, a few benches, a rough desk for the key man, possibly a couple of packing company telephones (for their own use) a water cooler outside, and a smaller, elevated, screened-in "office" for the weighmaster.

The weighmaster had a row of windows in front of his long workbench and if he was lucky he could see cattle on the scale. Most of the time the windows were almost impossible to see through because of the dust and manure that splashed on them. He sat on a rough bench built of heavy lumber (usually with several cushions on it) and during heavy runs he might have to sit there for twelve or fourteen hours. The scale beam was on the table in front of him and he was busy weighing cattle, writing shippers' and buyers' names, prices and weights on the scale tickets, stamping weights on the tickets and pulling the rope or wire that rang the gong that signaled the counter that the cattle had been weighed and could be counted off the scale. After a certain number of drafts, or no more than fifteen minutes, he rang the gong several times rapidly to signal that it was time to balance the scales and to keep cattle off until he balanced them, an operation that took a couple of minutes or so.

Most scales had a piece of large water pipe that ran from the front of the scales to the weighmaster's office. This pipe was about head high to a man and was used as a speaking tube for the weigher to call the names and prices into the weighmaster. Another tube was used to call the buyers' names to the counter. Bob Caver, who was a weighmaster at number six scale, was a tinkerer and inventor. He rigged up an electric speaker system at number six and used it for several years before similar systems were put in at the other scales. Bob also rigged up several other inventions, including a device that stamped commission companies' and regular buyers' names on scale tickets. This system saved lots of writing time.

After the weighmaster had weighed thirty or forty drafts of cattle, the counter came into the scale office and the pen numbers were recorded on the tickets. The key man took his copy of the scale tickets (other copies went to the commission company office) and recorded the buyers' names and pen numbers in his book, then sorted the tickets with a stack to each of the major packers and a stack for the other buyers. Any time after this paperwork was done he was ready to turn cattle over to the buyer. Usually we pushed the key man enough that it really wasn't as slow as it might sound. All this paperwork was necessary although it sounds like it was overdone.

There was a man who worked for the Stockyards Company who had seniority enough to hold almost any position, but just didn't have enough on the ball to hold onto a job. The union required the Yard company to allow any man who had seniority to try out for any job that was open, and if the man could handle the job, then it was his. I remember once when he applied for a counter's job at number three. This was during a heavy run and he fouled up the scales so badly by ordering cattle in the wrong pens and miscounting them that the scales were shut down two or three hours every day to get the cattle re-sorted. This often-times required the help of the buyers or salesmen. Fortunately for everyone concerned, this man was moved on to another job.

Since scale houses had the only stoves on the Yards, they were quite popular in the wintertime. It always seemed that the

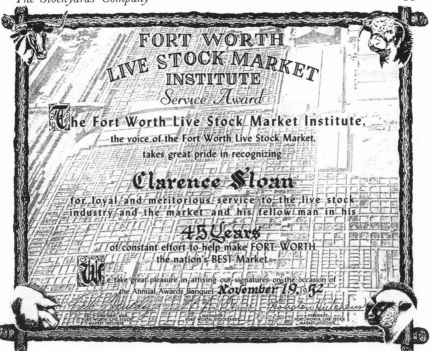

Certificate given to Clarence Sloan by Fort Worth Livestock Market Institute.

Cattle being counted off at number one scale. Photo courtesy of The Cattelman *magazine.*

temperature was at least two hundred degrees within five feet of the stove, but a lot less ten feet away.

B.M. Kerlee was foreman of the pen cleaning crew and his was a neverending job. He had a crew of twelve or fifteen men, six or eight trucks, and two tractors with bucket loaders. They also had a couple of small farm tractors that pulled a train of four-wheel dump carts. These carts would trail each other and it was funny to watch a tractor pull a train of six or eight carts into a pen, circle around and pass the last car in his train coming into the pen as the tractor was going out. All the manure was hauled north of 28th Street where it was dumped into a pile that covered about half a city block, twenty to thirty feet deep. Occasionally the manure pile would catch fire due to spontaneous combustion, but so much of it was wet that all it did was smolder and there was never any damage. Mr. Kerlee was an expert fiddle player and was in great demand for square dances.

The lawn in front of the Building was as pretty and well kept as any lawn anywhere. John Bobo (the father of all the Bobos on the Yards) worked for the Stockyards Company and spent all his time tending to the lawn and flowerbeds. Needless to say, he had plenty of fertilizer. Regardless of how much work is done on the new lawn, it will never be as pretty or have the care that Mr. Bobo gave the old one.

A.G. Donovan was manager of the stockyards when I first went to work there. Later, Bill Pier was in charge and the last man in charge while I was there was John Lewis. Bill Joyce and Elmo Klingenberg were assistant managers at one time or another. Walter Rice was public relations man and Tommy Hard was secretary of the company.

Sometime in the early fifties the Livestock Market Institute was formed by Ted Gouldy and several others representing the stockyards company, commission companies and order buyers. One of its purposes was to promote the Fort Worth Stockyards and its services. There were about twenty or thirty of us who were active in the organization. We held meetings about once a month, usually in one of the nicer restaurants around Fort Worth. To improve ourselves and be able to speak to the public, if necessary, we took a Dale Carnegie course so that we would be better qualified to promote the Yards.

[6]

Packers

All of the packing houses were referred to as "packers," and all of their buyers were "packer buyers." Swift and Armour, the largest, had six or eight buyers each on the cattle yards and some on the sheep and hog yards. The smaller packers like Bluebonnet, City Packing Company, Dallas City, Neuhoff, Rosenthal and others had only one or two buyers. In some cases the buyers for the smaller companies traded cattle on their own as well as buying for the packers. To my knowledge, this practice was not allowed by the larger packers.

Besides buyers on the Yards, Swift and Armour had their own crews to drive cattle from the scales to their holding pens and eventually to the packing houses. The smaller packers let their truck drivers gather cattle for them. Of course, the smaller packers might buy fewer than a hundred head per day, while Swift and Armour might buy a thousand or so each. Swift and Armour also had a junior buyer who was a buyer trainee and "caught weights" for them. The "weight catcher" went to the scales and recorded the weights of his company's buy for the day and phoned the total in to the packer's office on the packer's telephone in the scalehouse. These phones were an extension from the packer's office and for the use of the packers only, but sometimes you could find a new PBX operator in the office who would give you an outside line. On these occasions the phones could save a lot of steps.

I knew most of the packer buyers, but to this day I'm not certain who worked for which packer because Sloan rarely sold

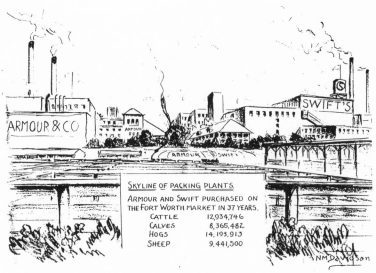

SKYLINE OF PACKING PLANTS.
ARMOUR AND SWIFT PURCHASED ON
THE FORT WORTH MARKET IN 37 YEARS.

CATTLE	12,934,746
CALVES	8,365,482
HOGS	14,193,913
SHEEP	9,441,500

N.M. Davidson drawing.

anything to the packers. Some of the buyers (on the cattle yards) were Ernest Swanzy, Jack Bourland, Johnny Walker, Lee Carrell, Herman Kennedy, Al Lowry, George Scaling, Bert O'Connell, Roy Weeman, Carl Reppeto, Harry Rosenthal, Jeff Minton, Herb Minton, Speck Fenner and Ray Shelton. Ray Shelton worked as a weight catcher as did Frank Bradley and Al Lowry, Jr.

The packers kept a lot of cattle in the red sheds and the extreme northwest area as well as the Q sheds. Sometimes they kept cutter and canner cows there for a couple of weeks until they were ready to use that type cattle. It was amazing to see the terrible condition and quality of some of the cows that the packers bought. There is no need to describe those cattle, but I still don't care to eat canned meat to this day.

Because of the size of their drives, the packers could cause traffic jams on the Yards when they were picking up cattle from the scales. If you were unlucky enough to get behind them when you were picking up, you were better off to go to the Building for a while and wait on them to get through. Most of us used sorting poles, canes or buggy whips to drive cattle, but the packers were required to use a "slapper" that was made of a couple of strips of heavy canvas with a wooden handle. The slapper wouldn't bruise cattle but made a slapping noise when you hit cattle with it. It was supposed to make cattle move faster, but I never knew it to do so.

All of the packers had "crip wagons" that were used to haul crippled cattle to the packing house. Any crippled or injured cattle were bought subject to inspection of the meat after they were butchered. These crip wagons were made of steel that rumbled and echoed like a drum. They were pulled with a tractor at high speed by low-paid help. They made as much noise as some of the modern bands and could be heard a long way off. The only difference between a crip wagon and a dead wagon used by the rendering plants was the condition of the cargo.

[7]

Theft

In preparing this book, I let several old hands read the manuscript before it was printed. One said the book was fine except that I should have deleted this chapter because of the subject. The subject is one that none of us liked but we had to accept it, and I would rather tell it like it was than leave it up to the reader's imagination.

Everyone who worked on the Yards had to be bonded. This was supposed to prevent theft, but it was not always successful. Although the great majority of dealers and commissionmen on the Yards were honorable and trustworthy, there were a very few who were not. I emphasize "few" because I never knew of more than three or four in the ten years I was there, and never saw a theft taking place.

Cow thieves didn't use a gun to steal stock, nor did they break into the Yards and drive off a full load of cattle at a time. In most cases they did not actually steal stock, but switched it. It would have been almost impossible to actually take an animal from the Yards because every animal that came in or out of the Yards was counted and recorded every time it changed ownership and numbers had to match or somebody was in trouble. There were cases where someone made errors in paperwork and cattle were actually taken from the Yards.

A favorite method of theft was to take a thin calf similar to a heavier one and switch them when no one was looking. Sometimes this was done in broad daylight while the packers were hold-

"Goober" Dickson, brand inspector, clipping hair to read a brand more clearly. N.M. Davidson drawing.

ing a large number of cattle in an alley, unattended. This method took a lot of nerve, which most of the thieves had plenty of anyway. The most popular way was to make the swap late in the afternoon or at night when no one was around to notice. This required a key or some other way, such as hitting the lock in the right place with a heavy walking cane or club, to open a gate. There was at least one key man I knew who would unlock any pen on the Yards for a couple of dollars. Because the number of cattle in a load was the same after the theft as before, it was hard to detect.

This worked best when cattle were in the shipping division in the care of the Stockyards Company, where they were rarely seen again by the shipper. But cattle were sometimes switched if they were left unattended in an alley for any length of time. One buyer for a small packer was driving cattle down an alley one day and met some cattle he had bought earlier in the day being driven in the opposite direction; they had been switched while he was picking up at a scale.

The switching technique worked best with the packing houses because the thieves would trade a sorry calf for a good one and since the packer buyer hardly ever saw his "buy" again after he had bought them from the commission company no one was the wiser. The thief had to be careful and not trade for a calf that was a lot heavier because his paperwork could show the correct number of cattle but would show an excessive weight gain that would draw suspicion from the office force.

In more than one case, several people worked together in switching cattle. Most of them were caught and fined and all of them were barred from trading on the Yards. One man was never caught in the act, although his actions were known to many and he was barred from trading. He became a very wealthy businessman on the North Side after leaving the Yards.

[8]

The Lay of the Land

The commission companies were located in the southern and eastern sections of the Yards and the order buyers and traders were in the northwestern section. The sheep and hog division as well as the horse and mule division were across Exchange Avenue in covered pens.

After a sale, the commission company had to weigh the cattle to the buyer. If the commission company had a first turn at the scale and if the cattle you bought were in pens handy to the scales, you could have your cattle weighed reasonably early. If not, you could wait several hours for your cattle, because they were usually weighed starting with the pens closest to the scales. If you bought cattle from several different pens at one commission company you might have to wait a long time for your cattle. Sometimes if you helped get the cattle to the scales, they would weigh them for you sooner. Multiply your buy by several commission companies and seven or more scales and it could take a long time and several trips to complete the pickup.

One scale would serve the several commission companies located closest to it. If one commission company had a very large run, they might move over to a scale that was not being used. Cattle were "picked up" from one to several times per day. To pick up, you planned a route from the scales where you had cattle, or at least where you knew your cattle were weighed. The scales were designated by the Stockyards Company with letters "A," "B," "C," "CC" (a double scale with "C"), "D," "E," "F," "G," and

'ROOMS'
TOTAL NUMBER ROOMS -2600
ALL PAVED
WITH RUNNING WATER-1800
TOTAL FLOOR SPACE
80 ACRES

N.M. Davidson drawing.

"Q." Except for "Q" and "CC," all the scales were known to everyone by a number (number one for "A," number two for "B," etc.).

All the pens and alleys on the Yards were numbered for identification. The east-west alleys were given even numbers (2, 4, 6, on up to 38 or 40) starting at Exchange Avenue. The north-south alleys were odd numbered, beginning with 1, starting at the railroad tracks on the east side of the Yards. "Main Alley" was the only alley that went all the way from Exchange Avenue to the drive-in gate near 28th Street. It was located just east of the Building.

All pens were given a number prefixed with the alley number the pens were located on, with even numbers on the right side of the alley and odd numbers on the left. For example, Sloan's pens were 30-24, 30-26, 30-28, 30-35, 30-37, 30-39, 30-41 and a couple around the corner on fifteen alley, 15-45 and 15-47. Catch pens at the scales were prefixed with the scale designation such as C-3, C-5, B-20, E-44, etc. Each scale except number four, which handled mostly large drafts of cattle, had probablyS a hundred or so catch pens, but they were all very small, some of them as small as ten by twelve feet. Most pens and smaller alleys in the commission companies' divisions were prefixed with the nearest scale's letter.

Every gate on every pen had a board for a sliding gate latch, a steel hook (like a screen door hook but about twelve inches long) and a couple of steel links that fit over an eyebolt in the fence to secure the lock. To aid in sorting, all pen gates swung the same direction. Every intersection of every alley had at least three gates hanging on separate corners. By opening or closing the proper gates, you could stop, continue on, or turn any direction at any intersection. There were also gates halfway between intersections. These were "block" gates that could be used to hold cattle, or to make an alley shorter for sorting cattle. If any of the gates were too short a hip knocker was added to allow the gate to close properly.

The city put a couple of water mains through the Yards in 1946 or '47 and in doing so they "butchered" several of the intersections where two alleys met, to make the intersections large enough for a fire truck to be able to turn a corner. This helped the fire trucks on their rare runs to the Yards, but it made it a lot more difficult to "set" gates to drive cattle. This may have been necessary for fire protection but it played the devil in lining gates. Ordinarily, it was no problem to keep cattle from running over you while you were setting gates at an intersection; after the intersections were widened to thirty or forty feet, however, you had to block cattle behind you to cross one of these intersections because cattle could get by you with that much room.

[9]

Moving 'em

There were several ways of driving cattle. One man could drive them by "setting" or "lining" the gates ahead of the cattle for several blocks, then walking back and driving the cattle ahead until they got to the end of the "lineup" he had made. There he would block a gate behind them and repeat the procedure to his destination. If two or more hands were driving cattle, one would set or line up the gates ahead of the cattle and the other would drive them. The smart driver would occasionally close a gate behind him so he didn't have to chase an animal too far if it turned back on him. More than once I've gotten lazy and not blocked a gate behind a drive, then had a long run to catch cattle that ran over me. It was unheard of to "break" a man's lineup intentionally. It was sometimes done accidentally, especially if a driver set the gates too far ahead and was not seen by the person going through the gate. We used the term "farmer" derogatorily when we referred to someone who left a gate open. Although there were walkways on nearly all the fences, we walked on them only when necessary because the alleys were so much faster to travel.

To climb to the walkways, there was a stairway of six or seven steps and a small gate with spring-loaded hinges to keep it shut. At about the same time as the intersections were widened, some bright soul decided that cattle could climb these steps and fall into the adjoining pen. This did happen a few times at night when cattle were being driven from the drive-in gate to the commission companies. The cattle were usually all accounted for and no harm

42

CHECKING OUT
GUESTS ENROUTE, BY RAIL AND TRUCKS
TO PASTURES, FEED LOTS OR PACKING
HOUSES IN OTHER CITIES.
38 STATES, FROM COAST TO COAST,
RECEIVED OUR FORMER GUESTS IN 1938.

The Drive-in Gate N.M. Davidson drawing.

was done, but the Stockyards Company removed the stairs and put ladders in their place. This stopped the cattle climbing, but it sure made it hard on the humans. Fortunately, these ladders were only put on the major north-south alleys.

Nearly everybody on the Yards carried a heavy walking cane, sorting pole or buggy whip for driving cattle. Quite a few hands used walking canes as an aid in setting gates. By using the crooked end as a hook, they could reach a little farther to pull a gate or to knock the gate hook open. Some hands practiced swinging a gate shut and throwing the hook at the right time to have it fall into its eye just as the gate closed. This was just one little diversion to kill time. All of these items were used to aid in sorting cattle. Sorting poles were the handiest item for sorting cattle but were easy to break and did not have a long life. Most salesmen used buggy whips to move cattle around to show them off. This was the only good use for a whip, because they were notorious for blinding cattle when a man tried to stop an animal by popping him on the nose, but hit him in the eye instead.

On a busy day, picking up could be a long drawn-out affair because several buyers all had the same idea and wanted to get their cattle picked up at the same time. If a buyer had a lot of hands they could move their cattle in separate groups, while other buyers had to put all their cattle in one or two bunches and sort them out after they had them in their division. Every commission company and buyer was allotted certain pens for their use but

could use others when theirs were all full. Shortly after the war-
time ceiling price was removed, there were more than twenty thousand cattle received at the Yards on one day. The commission
companies did not have enough pens and spilled over into the
buyers' division. The buyers had no place to put the cattle they
bought until the commission companies sold their cattle and moved
out of the buyers' pens, a real vicious circle. On some occasions
the sheep yards would have to send their overflow to pens on the
cattle yards.

Most of the hands who worked for the buyers hated number
five scale because it was the farthest away from the buyers' division. You had to be sure that every head was picked up because
you did not knowingly leave an animal overnight in the catch pens
at the scale for any reason. Sometimes they were left by accident
but never on purpose. When you picked up your cattle you kept
a record of them and their weights by copying the information
from the scale tickets. Sometimes traffic jams could really be a
problem when several buyers were picking up along with the packers and you might have to wait an hour or so to get through it.
Sometimes you would have to take an alternate route and almost
circle the entire yards before you got to your division.

If you were trying to pick up cattle alone you had to walk
twice as far, because you had to line gates for some distance ahead
of your cattle, then walk back and drive them ahead. Sometimes
you could tag along behind someone else who was going your way
and sometimes you could return the favor by letting someone follow
you. Of course, you would set the gates behind you to turn him
into his division. At other times you simply combined cattle with
someone else to make the drive simpler. This worked best when
you had just a few head.

If a trader were buying for several customers at once, it might
be necessary to keep each customer's cattle separate when you
picked up. This could add to the confusion, but it could also eliminate a lot of sorting later on.

It was essential to keep hay picked up off the ground at all
times because hay was expensive, necessary for weight gain, and
cattle would not eat it when it was dirty. It also had to be fluffed
up to make it more palatable to the cattle.

When all the cattle were shaped up into carloads they were
held in the pens long enough to fill so long as they weren't obvi-

ously stuffed, and then were weighed to the order buyer's customer. They were taken to scale number four and weighed, then
Stockyards Company hands took possession of them and drove
them to the shipping division.

If it was necessary (and it usually was) to vaccinate the cattle
being shipped, or brand them, you turned them over to the branding
chute, which was run by an individual approved by the Stockyards Company. To operate, the operator paid the Stockyards Company a percentage of the fees (which were set by the company).
In most cases these things were done after the cattle were weighed
and in care of the Stockyards Company. The cattle had to be inspected by Federal health inspectors who never worked past four
in the afternoon, and most of the railroads did not start loading
out until eight or so at night, so there was at least a four- or
five-hour period that the branding chute crew had to work on
cattle being shipped. Other cattle might be worked on until midnight.

After this, you could go home unless the Stockyards Company was late in cleaning your pens, then it meant manning a
shovel for a while. But the shovel could be the start of something
big because most of the commissionmen and buyers started out
on the end of a shovel and worked their way through all the jobs
to the top. Some of them eventually owned the company they started
working for many years before. A lot of them worked for nearly
everybody on the Yards at one time or another.

Shippers sent their cattle to the Yards in every imaginable
type of truck or trailer. All big trucks, that is, semitrailers (which
at that time only had ten wheels instead of eighteen), were factory
made. Very few if any two-wheeled trailers were factory made,
partly because of the war and partly because no factory had ever
started producing them. Nearly all of them were homemade or
made in the local blacksmith shop. (That's right, blacksmith shop.
Welding shops weren't in existence yet.) There were no standards
that trailers had to conform to and as a result there were very
few built alike. If someone designed a trailer that pulled well and
handled well, others copied it. Pulling a two-wheeled trailer with
a couple of big cows or bulls in it behind a pickup overloaded
with cows could be real dangerous when the cattle moved around
a little in the trailer. After the war when people learned to put
two axles under trailers and build them lower to the ground, and

were able to buy heavier pickups to pull them, the safety factor was much better.

When a whole herd of cattle is being shipped it is necessary to have enough trucks to haul all the cattle at one time to prevent weight loss. Only a few trucking companies had enough trucks to haul some of the larger shipments, so a lot of them helped each other on big jobs when fifteen or twenty trucks might be needed.

There were several trucking businesses around the Yards. They operated much like the commission companies and order buyers in that some of the truck company owners had at one time worked for the company they later owned, and most truck drivers had at one time or another worked for nearly all the truck lines. Some truckers had one or two trucks, while others had a dozen or more. Nowadays, one cattle truck can haul what two or three could haul in the forties. Some of the truckers were Henry Johnson, Slim Massey, Yount-Hart, George Russey, Graves & Ryon, and Paul Healy. Henry Johnson was the first trucker to buy new trucks after the war. Somehow Henry managed to buy five new Dodge trucks and trailers before any of the other truckers could.

Healy Motor Lines was the biggest for many years and hauled most of Sloan's cattle. Some truckers had the reputation of never being on time, their drivers stopping for coffee with a truck full of cattle, and other problems. I once saw three trucks loaded with cattle on the way to the scales stop at a grocery store because one of the drivers had run out of cigarettes. All of this was bad news, because a load of cattle being hauled from a ranch to the scales loses weight by the minute, and the loss could amount to several dollars per load even at 1945 prices.

Paul Healy and his wife were on their way to a party one night when he saw one of his trucks loaded with cattle, parked at a beer joint. He sent his wife on to the party and took the truck to its destination, still dressed in his party clothes. Needless to say, when the driver came out of the joint, he had no job. This was the kind of service Paul provided, so it's easy to see why he had the largest trucking business. A lot of the smaller, one-truck truckers provided the same service, but they only had one truck and could not haul a great number of cattle at a time. George Russey was another trucker who gave outstanding service and hauled a lot of cattle.

[10]

Personalities

It may seem unusual to some that I have named in the dedication of this book more than four hundred people that I worked with. There were at least another hundred who worked for the packers and Stockyards Company that I did not know by name, and a least a hundred more who were regular customers and shippers. Counting everybody, there were at least three hundred people at work on the Yards at any time.

When you were waiting for cattle to be weighed, you might spend time at a commission company booth, where some of their shippers might be waiting also. It was no problem to start a conversation with these people, who may have been ordinary cowboys or big ranch owners or managers and may have been from any part of Texas, Oklahoma or New Mexico. You might also meet buyers from California, Nebraska, Kansas, Kentucky, or anywhere in the United States. You could learn a lot by meeting and visiting with these people or standing back and listening in on conversations. This was also an opportunity to make contacts that could help you in the future. On top of that, you could pick up some pretty juicy gossip.

C. Sloan shipped so many loads of cattle on the Texas and Pacific, Katy, Missouri Pacific and other railroads that he was often called on by some of the visiting officials of the roads. Once, Matthew Sloan (no kin), president of the Katy, was in Fort Worth and came to the Yards to visit. Matthew Sloan was a very wealthy man. When he was introduced to C. Sloan, he asked if Clarence

When Paul Whiteman bought a load of cattle for Swift & Company 1937 l. to r. Clarence Sloan, Paul Whiteman, Bill Sloan, Bert O'Connell, (head buyer for Swift), Bevins Callan, salesman for Texas Livestock Marketing Association. Fort Worth Star-Telegram photo.

spelled Sloan with an "e" on it. C. Sloan replied that he didn't and Matthew Sloan said that he didn't either and that you weren't supposed to add the "e" until you had made a million dollars. So far, I'm still working on my "e."

Clarence Sloan had a lot of customers in North and West Texas who bought steer and heifer yearlings every year in September and October and grazed them on wheat pasture until May or June, when they resold them. Sometimes Sloan would buy them back to ship to other customers in the East. We had a lot of customers from all over North Texas who bought hundreds of cattle every fall. One customer, Roscoe Edwards at Stoneburg, had an inflexible rule that he followed every year. When he sold his cattle in June for, say two hundred twenty dollars per head, he would replace them with two head in October that cost no more than two hundred twenty dollars for the pair. He stuck with this rule as long as I knew him. In some years he had to replace with some pretty sorry cattle to meet his price, but other years he could buy the best quality. I guess this rule worked pretty well because he was pretty well off when he died.

John Young of Megargel was a longtime customer of Sloan's and his sons became good customers, too. John A. Young, Jr., was working on a pilot's license when I first met him in 1945. He wanted to buy an airplane to get enough time to complete his license, so I took him out to Hicks Field where he bought a surplus L4 (Piper Cub) for fifteen hundred dollars. Since he had never flown a Cub, he asked me to fly him home to Seymour that afternoon and ride back on the bus the next day. It was a little late when we left Hicks with the plane and by the time we got close to Megargel daylight was just about gone, so he pointed out his father's farm where we landed and spent the night. He didn't tell me about the telephone line across the field until after we had landed. If he had told me about it I doubt that I would have tried to land, but everything worked out fine.

The next day he wanted to show off his plane, so he had me fly him all over Baylor County to the farms of friends and relatives. I had to take somebody up at every stop and there were about ten stops before noon. He was having so much fun with his airplane that we flew on back to Fort Worth instead of riding the bus. John A. and his brother Pat both got their private pilot's licenses with this plane, kept it several years and sold it for several hundred dollars more than John A. paid for it. L.C. Young of Graham was a brother of John A.'s and a longtime customer, as was John A.'s brother-in-law, Charlie Porter of Seymour.

My father, Clarence Sloan, was active on the Yards for fifty years or so and I am proud of the fact that he did as much as anyone else to build the Yards. He would turn over in his grave if he thought I was writing this, because he was the type who kept out of the limelight and tended to his own business, but he was not alone in this respect, as most of the people on the Yards felt the same way.

D.G. "Pinky" Talbot was a man who put honor and reputation above money. He sold an auction barn that he owned over in East Texas and the new owners made some deals that reflected on Pinky's honor. Pinky paid off the debts of the new owners even though he was not legally obligated to do so. He felt he was morally bound though it was said to have cost him over fifty thousand, 1950s' dollars. Pinky was an A&M graduate and had been a colonel in the tank corps in Africa during World War II and had been awarded several medals. He was once written up in war correspondent Ernie Pyle's newspaper column, which was quite an honor in itself. Pinky was not a regular at the Yards, although he did a lot of trading there, but he is an example of the type men we had. Not all men were as honorable as Pinky, but I know of several other similar, though not as costly, cases.

The people who worked on the Yards in all capacities covered the social spectrum. Several were not much more than winos living from day to day. At the other end of the scale, there were those whose names were on the membership rolls of Rivercrest and Colonial country clubs as well as the Fort Worth Club.

Several owned or leased farms or pastures because most of them ran cattle outside of their business on the Yards. Some who were just starting out might have to go thirty miles or so to lease a pasture where they could run about a dozen head. These pastures made the operators money, because it gave them a place to keep bargain-priced cattle as they bought them.

One man on the Yards, a member of a pioneer family, lived in Parker County and commuted to the Yards daily. He was a frugal man; to pay his way, he sold and delivered eggs from his ranch to the cafes in the area around four a.m. every morning. The commission company he worked for had trouble balancing its books and discovered that this man had not cashed his paychecks for nearly a year. It was said that he would fold a one hundred dollar bill so that only a one showed, and put it in his church's collection plate several times per year.

When I say that some of the people were tough, I mean that a few people on the Yards had killed men in the past, but in most of the cases it was self-defense. At least one of the outlaws who was found full of holes in the Lake Worth area worked on the Yards, and the Corner was the hangout for a lot of the outlaws of the era.

One man who had worked on the Yards for a short time, and left several years before my time, was working on the San Antonio Yards as a buyer. This man had a girlfriend who had left him for a soldier from Fort Hood. He got a lot more than even with the man who took his girl because he and a friend found the girlfriend with the soldier one afternoon, and castrated the soldier. This was pretty effective punishment, but let the punishment fit the crime.

Regardless of all the television commercials about how acceptable it is to drink all the beer you want while you are on the job, that rule did not apply on the Yards in my time and before. Not that people did not drink, for a lot of them did, and did a lot of it, but it was not allowed to mix with business. I have seen hands fired on the spot because they had a beer or two at lunch. If a hand showed up for work "hung over" on Monday morning or did not show up at all because of drinking, that was "all she wrote" and the hand was looking for another job. Though some hands hid their drinking as much as possible they were still found out. Any hand who had a reputation for drinking did not last long. There were exceptions to this and there were several drinkers who kept their bottles hidden in hay mangers.

All the current controversy over liquor laws, open containers, etc., seems silly to me, because I knew some pretty tough people back in the forties and fifties and there was not a one of them who did not respect and obey most of the liquor laws. They were very careful to not have any open containers in the car with them, and even kept sealed bottles out of sight. Nor would they take more than their quota of alcohol into a dry county, not because they were angels, but because they knew that breaking the law carried stiff penalties that would be enforced.

Although the commissionmen and buyers frowned on hands drinking, there were some of them who were professional drinkers, but they worked for themselves and most didn't stay in the cattle business too long. There were some exceptions, however, who lasted many years. Some wound up as winos on the Corner and were really pitiful to see, especially those who were at one time among the biggest operators on the Yards. I personally saw one trader go from a pretty good operation, through a few barrels of whiskey, another man's wife, and a lot of money, and wind up as a cowboy on a ranch in West Texas in a few, short years. C. Sloan had a saying that "every man is entitled to nine barrels of whiskey. I had mine and quit." I never knew him to take a drink.

Everyday language on the Yards was pretty rough. There were a few men who had not completed high school, but even the crudest hands had better grammar than we are accustomed to today. One phrase that was used universally was "son of a bitch." It was used as a noun, adjective, verb, adverb, or anything else and pronounced as one word. It could be meant as a great compliment or sometimes in its common use as a derogatory term.

Police brutality existed at the time but we didn't know there was a name for it. I have seen winos nearly beaten to death being loaded in a police car at the Corner. I think their "Sweet Lucy" cost something like forty-nine cents a quart and a quart could knock out two or three of them. I have seen them in all stages of drunkenness all over Exchange Avenue and its alleys.

Hardly a weekend went by without a shooting or stabbing somewhere around the Corner. I did not see any of these firsthand, because I did not get anywhere close to that area after dark, but I heard these things from some of the hands who did hang out there, and saw quite a few unconscious bodies on the sidewalks on Sunday mornings when I went to the Yards to feed.

Although the police may have been a little rough on the winos, more than once I have seen the police bring in a load of cattle after they had stopped a truck driver for DWI, and I know of one case where they had seen a truckload of cattle stopped at a beer joint for a couple of hours, so they located the driver in the beer joint, took him to jail and took the cattle to the Yards because they knew that the cattle were not supposed to be treated like that. I'm sure this was beyond the call of duty, but they saw something that needed to be corrected and did it. Nowadays, I'm sure someone's rights would surely have been violated.

I doubt if the Yards, as I knew it, could even operate under today's restrictions of OSHA, constitutional rights, civil rights, animal rights, minimum wage, etc. People were hired and fired on the spot. A forty-hour, five-day week was unheard of (I saw our house in the daylight only on Sunday afternoons for a three-or four-week period in the late forties). On normal Saturdays and Sundays the yard hands took turns going by the pens early and late in the day to feed and water the cattle. The cattle had to be tended to whether it was Christmas, Thanksgiving or Sunday.

Although it happened in the early thirties and was before my time, it may be of interest to know that there was an attempted bank robbery at the Corner by a bandit with a bottle of nitroglycerin. Some way or another he dropped the bottle and killed himself and I think a couple of others. I'm not sure, but I think it was The Stockyards National Bank at that time and was located at the corner of Exchange and the alley that was on the west side of the coliseum. The North Fort Worth State Bank used this building during the forties. Shorty Russey, who worked on the Yards when I was there, had been an ambulance driver for Shannon's at the time of the holdup and told me the gory details of picking up the pieces. There were several shootings and knifings on Exchange in my time and it was far from the showplace of today.

The merchants in the area today may hate me for this, but I saw and heard enough in my day that I still wouldn't care to go out on West Exchange after dark and I would be a little edgy on East Exchange. I don't know what the attraction was, but a lot of outlaws congregated around the Corner. Some of them had businesses there and others just hung around.

Raymond Hamilton (Clyde Barrow's buddy in the thirties) had a sister who owned a liquor store on Exchange. Tincy Eggleston, who was quite notorious during the forties and fifties and was shot and dumped in a well near Saginaw, owned a barn and some pens on North Houston just off Exchange where he traded horses. A few times I helped catch horses that had gotten away from his barn. Tincy, among others, had an interest in some of the gambling joints on the Corner. Dick Nowlin, a calf salesman on the Yards, was a "dead ringer" for Tincy except Dick's hair was a lighter color. I'm sure Dick felt a little safer after Tincy was gone.

One man who had been tough in the early days was Pony Starr. Pony worked around the Yards for a short time for C. Sloan and others in the twenties and thirties. Pony killed several men in a famous shootout near Porum, Oklahoma. Pony gave C. Sloan an odd-shaped rock that he had carried for a lucky charm during that shootout. I understand that he gave some other items to a couple of other men on the Yards. Pony was a cousin of Henry Starr, the infamous Oklahoma outlaw. I remember going with the family to visit Pony and his wife in the thirties when he lived near Smithfield. The last time I saw him was shortly before he died about 1946 or '47.

One of the cattle dealers from the Yards was connected with a gambling operation in Haltom City during the fifties. He hired several hands from the Yards to be guards for the establishment and it was funny to a lot of us to see them acting as guards because we didn't think most of them were tough enough for that business. I know that it wasn't funny to them though, because things were pretty rough during that time. This trader was approached by someone in the Haltom City fire department to make a donation for a new fire truck. The trader, being a generous type, thought this was a good cause so he bought a completely equipped truck for the fire department. The good citizens of Haltom City were in an uproar when they found out where the truck came from and tried to have him indicted for making a payoff. I guess they wouldn't have said a word if the money had gone to a public official under the counter. This man had to take the truck back and later used it as a cattle sprayer.

Quite a few men on the Yards had violent tempers. Everybody knew who they were and gave them plenty of room. Clarence Sloan was known for his temper and very few ever crossed him — one exception was a "mouthing" drunk he knocked off a fence with a water pole. Harry Fifer also had a short fuse. In the early part of World War II, a delivery man, who was a member of some religious cult that did not believe in saluting the flag, made some remark about not standing or saluting the flag. About two seconds later the man was on the floor of the Building, missing a few teeth. I don't know who won, though, because Fifer's hand got infected and he had a lot of trouble with it.

Several years later at a meeting of the Livestock Market Institute, Fifer was griping (good-naturedly) because Clint Shirley had been served a steak earlier than Fifer. The owner of the restaurant, who was a little cocky, heard of the complaint from one of the waitresses and proceeded to tell Fifer that he was getting good service and to quit complaining. In a lot less time than it takes to read this Fifer (who was over six feet) had the restaurant owner (who was a lot smaller) lifted off the floor and up to Fifer's eye level where he proceeded to tell the owner how to run the restaurant properly. If Fifer had hit him it would have been rough, but he lowered him to the floor and that was all of it. The service had been a little slow, but not all that bad. After the incident, you wouldn't believe how many waitresses showed up and how fast the rest of us got to eat.

There were a few marital triangles around the Yards, as there were everywhere else. Some of the men considered themselves God's gift to women and were after all of them. There was probably as much hanky-panky going on then as now, but it was a lot quieter. Some yard hands showed me bullet holes that had been put in them by jealous husbands or boyfriends.

There were several couples who met and married while working at the Yards. Among these were Carnell and Allen Thompson, Patsy and Harold Harrison, Frances and Dean Chester, Evelyn and Walter Graves. There were several other couples who worked on the Yards.

Roger Muncy and, I believe, Bill Martin conned me into escorting a girlfriend of their wives to a dance with them and several other couples. I knew that this girl was married and her husband was in Korea, but they told me that everything was all right because this girl was a close friend of their wives and needed to get out of the house. So being good hearted, willing to help them out and knowing that everybody understood the situation, I invited the girl to the dance. While we were at the dance, Bill and Roger informed me that her husband had just come back from Korea and was due in town that night. Of course he hadn't, but it sure ruined the night for me since I hadn't wanted to take out a married woman in the first place and never took out another one in the second place.

In all my years at the Yards I only dated three or four girls in the Building. There were several very attractive girls in the offices but unfortunately most of them were either married or too old for me. I would have tried to date more, but I just didn't want to face the teasing that took place around the building.

I dated the daughter of a commissionman a few times and on one of our last dates, her three year old niece was staying with the family. When I was about to leave, the niece, who had a lot of conversation for her age, told me that I didn't have to leave, that they had a lot of room and I could sleep with Mary Jo. It took me a couple of weeks to get the nerve to call Mary Jo again.

Just because I didn't go out with many girls from the Yards didn't mean that I didn't get around at all. I did my share of chasing the girls, but didn't catch very many. Having to be at the Yards at six in the morning discouraged keeping late hours too often. I found that socializing required too much drinking to suit me. I never did determine if they were drinking to stand me or each other.

Sometime around 1950 a girl who could win any beauty contest hands down went to work in one of the offices. Any time this girl walked in the lobby every male eye followed her. She had the looks and dressed stylishly. She only worked there for about a month or so and a strong rumor was that she was willing to live with any man for one hundred dollars per week, for a week only, nights only and no housework. One hand claimed to have done this, but the rest of us wondered and wondered and wondered.

One real unfortunate incident that happened was the case of a man who worked on the sheep yards becoming infatuated with a girl who worked in the Western Union office. This man had a family but that made no difference to him. The girl was transferred to another office to avoid the man, but he simply went to the new office and hung around her. Because she would have nothing to do with him, he waited on a downtown street for her to pass on her way home from work and shot her. He shot himself but recovered.

[11]

The Garb

If there was a standard dress for the Yards, it was either khaki pants and khaki shirt or Levi's and khaki shirt, or either with a gray Carl Pool shirt most of the year, and gray wool western pants and jackets in the winter. Notice that I said "Levi's." Never, never, were they called "jeans." Probably ninety percent of the people on the Yards wore khakis or Levi's most of the time. Levi's as well as other types of clothes were scarce during the war. Seymour Drescher, who owned the White Front Store, or his son-in-law Morris Schwartz, always provided me and several others with a couple of pairs of Levi's every three or four months during the shortage.

Some of the people wore boots a lot of the time, but everybody experimented with nearly every kind of footwear imaginable, because those old bricks could wear out your feet as well as a pair of expensive boots in a hurry. Tennis shoes, work shoes, rubber soles, leather soles, high heels, low heels: We tried them all except hippie sandals. Among the longest wearing and most comfortable to me were war surplus GI combat boots. Quite a few people wore them until the surplus stores ran out. Footwear was extremely important because of the amount of walking. I checked our mileage with a pedometer (it was my old Jack Armstrong Hike-O-Meter) and discovered that we were walking about fifteen miles on an average day. That covers a lot of bricks.

Everybody kept raincoats or rainsuits in their booths and you could always find an extra pair of pants or shirt in a booth be-

"Texas" Yard crew and salesmen l. to r. Bob Gibson, Billy Emmons, Ed Nelson, Sidney Jenkins, Alonzo Keen, Roy Boswell, C.L. Keen. Photo courtesy Sid Jenkins.

Jim Corley, J.D. Tadlock, Wade Choate, Sidney Jenkins. Note typical dress also cane and sorting pole. Photo courtesy Sid Jenkins.

cause you never knew when you were going to rip or tear something and you might not have the time to go to Seymour's or Samuel Sheinberg's for another pair. Levi's were Levi's in those days. You had a choice of blue or blue and if you didn't wash them a couple of times before you first wore them, you turned blue and they rubbed you raw. There never was anything more painful than having a case of adult diaper rash caused by a new pair of Levi's. They seemed to be considerably thicker than they are now and a lot stiffer. You could not wash them the first couple of times with anything else because the blue dye would color anything within miles. Levi's sold for $3.45 a pair before the ceilings on prices were removed, then they went to $3.95.

While we are on the subject of dress I might mention that the men from the Yards were not afraid to dress up. You can't imagine the difference clothes made on a man unless you have been used to seeing him in his work clothes, usually dusty and dirty, and then see him at some social function. Once, when we had a meeting of the Livestock Market Institute, I almost had to ask who some of the men were. I had worked all day with them, but had never seen them dressed up. Quite a few of the older men wore suits complete with neckties all of the time. Big hats were common, of course, but snap brims were worn by at least a fourth of the men.

Another item along the same lines: More than once boys with hair a little too long to suit their peers were given free haircuts by some of those peers. Today, there would surely be a lawsuit over something like that. I have often wondered if the long hair and whiskers of today would have been accepted on the Yards. If the longhairs had been exposed to the elements, the sweat, and the unbelievable amount of dust (which was nothing but powdered manure) we were exposed to, I believe they would have changed their style. When a yard hand left the Yards to go out on the town, he made certain that he was clean and was wearing clean clothes and polished boots or shoes. No sweat-stained hats or torn clothes. There were a few exceptions to this, but they wouldn't have dressed for any occasion.

Although khaki or chambray shirts were worn to work most of the time, most of the younger hands had to have Jack McClure or some other shirtmaker custom make shirts for rodeoing. I doubt that anyone under the influence of the pills they take today could dream up the wild colors and patterns that were worn in those days. It seemed that there was no pattern or color that was too wild for Saturday night rodeos.

Jack McClure was a tailor and made shirts for lots of rodeo hands. The well-dressed yard hand or rodeo hand had to have tailor-made shirts. Tailor-made shirts certainly cost more than regular ones, but there was some prestige about them and you could have them made out of any material you were brave enough to wear. Jack had tailor shops in various locations around the Corner and must have made thousands of shirts. At that time I think tailor-made shirts were about $7.50 and up, while work shirts were a couple of dollars. Before Jack started in business, Harris Tailoring Shop made most of the shirts.

Sloan always wore clothes that blended in with the surroundings and he could disappear from sight if you blinked. Many times I have stood next to him, looked off for a minute and when I turned back he would be gone. His idea was that I was supposed to keep up with him instead of him telling me where he was going. On some of these disappearances I would find him sitting in a hay manger with a salesman looking at a bunch of cattle.

The way a person wore his hat or clothes had an effect on the way he was accepted on the Yards. If someone wore a hat tilted too far back or to one side, he was looked on by his peers as being a little strange. Some people always wore their hats with a distinctive crease and they could be spotted a long way off by the look of their hat. During rainy weather when everybody was wearing the same type rainsuit, you could spot a man by his hat. There were others that would not crease their hat differently from the crowd so that their hat wouldn't give them away if they were seen in the wrong place at the wrong time. Quite a few would not put their name or initials in their hats for the same reason.

If a man didn't wear a hat at all, it usually took him a little longer to be accepted. I knew of one man who was hired as manager of one of the largest ranches in the country, but did not keep the job too long because the cowboys couldn't accept the fact that he went bareheaded most of the time. There weren't over two or three people that I remember who went bareheaded, and they wore hats part of the time.

Quite a few hands went without shirts during the summer months and some turned pretty brown. Although a few hands went in the Building without a shirt, it was frowned on, so most of them always had a shirt handy to wear in the Building. Very few broke this unwritten rule. How times have changed.

[12]

Cowboys and cowboys

The name "cowboy" was used in as many variations as "son of a bitch." With a small c, it could be used to describe an unacceptable way of handling cattle. Being referred to as a Cowboy, on the other hand, could be the greatest compliment a man could be paid. I have known lots of Cowboys and cowboys but never knew of anyone who admitted to being either.

Wild cattle are harder to handle in the Eastern States than they are in Texas. C. Sloan once got a telegram in the mid-thirties from a customer in Virginia: "Please send six Texas cowboys by airplane, last load of cattle seen headed for Texas." They finally found them, but at the time no one in Virginia knew how to handle cattle except on foot, and range cattle cannot be handled except on horseback. They were in a part of Virginia that used rail fences almost exclusively and of course the cattle could jump them as well as the Virginian's fox hunting horses could. The cattle were finally caught without the airmail shipment of cowboys but they were scattered over a pretty big area of Virginia.

Some men participated in major rodeos and many more participated in the Saturday night rodeos scattered around the area. A lot of them were topnotch hands. Some of the hands who rodeoed were George Wilderspin, J.D. Tadlock, Mike Ward, Mike Walters, Speck McLaughlin, Red Jaquess, Frank Quirk, Wayne Stewart, Bill Yeary, Goldie Corbin, Jake Corbin, Hilton Kutch, Joe Reppeto, L.T. McCoy, Roger Muncy, Lloyd McBee, Ed Barnett, Bill Gardenhier, Roy Barton, Jack Matthews, Leroy Bobo, Bill

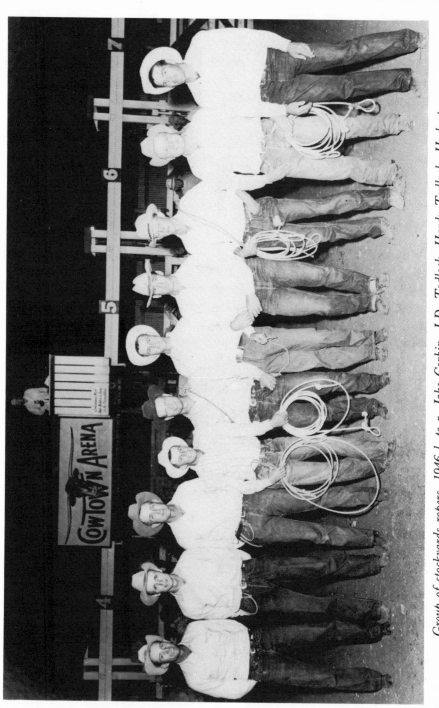

Group of stockyards ropers, 1946 l. to r. Jake Corbin, J.D. Tadlock, Hardy Tadlock, Herbert Straw, J.P. Bobo, John "Tiger" Hosea, Bill Yeary, Windy Ryon, Bill Iler. Photo by Bill Sloan.

Martin, Herbert Straw, George Willoughby, Charley Woods, J.R. Bettis, Ward Lindsey, Peewee Nix, Happy Skaggs, Guy Baugh, Guy Harrell, Gus Davidson, Charley Poynor, Lou Quirk, Windy Ryon, Bubba Thomason, Hardy Tadlock, Charley Thomason, George Murray and me.

The calf ropers would use any excuse to promote a calf roping, and many team ropings were organized on the flimsiest excuses. Some were held at the Cowtown Arena, among others, and at the Avondale Roundup held at Hardy Tadlock's arena.

I saw George Wilderspin rope a calf at the Ponder Rodeo sometime around 1947 in eight seconds flat. This record stood for many, many years.

Although rodeoing was and is considered to be a cowboy sport, it was not looked on with much favor by the commissionmen and order buyers because of the danger of a yard hand getting hurt. A drinking, rodeoing yard hand could not look forward to a very long employment on the Yards, because sooner or later he was apt to show up on Monday morning crippled up. Don't get the idea that rodeoing was outlawed; most men enjoyed it so long as someone other than their hired hands was participating.

Quite a few of the younger hands on the Yards rodeoed in some fashion at some time. A lot of them rodeoed under fictitious names to prevent word getting back to the boss about their activities.

Sometime in the late forties, a group of North Side men including Pinky Straw, Hap Hovencamp, Carlton Lynch, J.T. Boothman and others, built a very nice rodeo arena just east of the intersection of North Main and 33rd, where the old Buddie's Supermarket was located. This was called the Cowtown Rodeo and first-class rodeos were held there for several years. I believe Dan Coates was the first announcer and later Porter Randal took over. Before this arena was built, most of the Saturday night rodeos were held at the Pecan Street arena, which was located a few blocks east of the present Seminary South Shopping Center. Even earlier there was an arena in Cobb Park. There were numerous Saturday night rodeos at Denton, Keller, Ponder, and a lot of other small towns.

You could find someone from the Yards at nearly all of the amateur rodeos in North Texas during the summer, at Henrietta, Seymour, Archer City, Mineral Wells, Stamford and many others.

Stockyards Roping Team "A" at Avondale Roundup 1948 l. to r. Wesley Cleveland, Ed Barnett, Hilton Kutch, Bill Sloan, Hardy Tadlock, George Willoughby, Jake Corbin. Bill Sloan photo.

Stockyards Roping Team "B" at Avondale Roundup 1948, l. to r. Murell Reese, Wayne Stewart, Mike Ward (winner) J.R. Bettis, J.D. Tadlock, Windy Ryon. Bill Sloan photo.

About half of the hands who rodeoed went to the amateur shows and the other half to the professional shows.

Nearly every year roping teams were formed and the hands got together and roped one team against the other. These ropings were mostly for fun because any excuse to have a roping was valid. Some of the ropings were held at Tadlock's during the annual Avondale Roundup, others at Saturday night rodeos.

Lloyd McBee and Leroy Bobo both worked for Sloan about 1945. Because of World War II there were no new cars to be had. Lloyd had bought a 1928 or '29 Buick that was in mint condition. He and Leroy made a trip in this car nearly to Canada, rodeoing. This was before he went to work for Sloan. Lloyd bragged that his old "deep breather" could pull his horse trailer over all kinds of mountains better than a new car. Leroy teased Lloyd about eating fried eggs three times a day. Lloyd said that a fried egg was one item of food he could look at and tell if it was spoiled.

Most of the younger hands (and a few older ones, too) felt they had a right to see the Fort Worth Stock Show Rodeo, free, every year. All sorts of schemes were hatched to be able to slip in to the rodeo. We gave all sorts of excuses to the guards why we didn't have a pass for our cars and it was fairly simple to get in and park free. Getting into the rodeo itself was another matter. Sometimes you could put your head down and walk in the back gate with the rodeo contestants, or help drive the stock, or sometimes you could con a guard with a sad story. One year I made it into eighteen of the nineteen performances at the stock show without paying a penny. I could have made all of them free but I had a date one night and couldn't slip her in. Several of the hands never missed a show for years.

The Cowtown Rodeo was a godsend for a lot of us because the first year they were in business they gave the contestants the same type and style of numbers to wear on their backs that the Stock Show Rodeo used. Since the numbers were made of heavy felt and would last a long time, several of us who rodeoed kept the numbers and from then on it was a snap to pin a number on your back and walk into the Stock Show Rodeo. At least it was a snap until a couple of years later when the Stock Show management changed the style of their numbers.

Another favorite trick was to borrow an official badge that had been issued to a superintendent or chute worker. This took a little extra work because someone who had a pass had to go in the arena and gather two or three badges to take outside to his buddies, then they could go in and return them to their owners. This was a surefire way when all other methods failed. I'm forever grateful to Bill Gardenhier for lending me a badge on many occasions.

Quite a few hands worked around the rodeos in various capacities. Louis Kubitz was stock manager for the Verne Elliott rodeo company and kept a lot of the rodeo stock pastured in the Fort Worth area between rodeos. One pasture where the rodeo stock was kept is now covered by the Ridgmar area. When I was in the cattle spraying business I sprayed the rodeo stock in that pasture many times. I also sprayed lots of cattle for A.C. Luther when the area around Luther Lake was nothing but pasture land and filled my sprayer many times from Luther Lake, one of Fort Worth's prettiest areas at Christmas. Wiley Alliston had a pasture where I sprayed many cattle that now is in the middle of the intersection of Interstate 30 and Highway 183.

The Edelbrock Saddle Shop on West Exchange made one of the best saddles that could be bought anywhere. Ed Chapman worked for Edelbrock's for forty years before retiring. I had Ed make a saddle for me in 1945, shortly after he opened his own shop, and it is as good now as when I bought it. When I had my saddle made, leather and saddle trees were scarce and I had to wait quite a while before Ed could get all the materials.

Most of the rodeo cowboys hung out at Edelbrock's during the stock show and I met quite a few of the top hands and rodeo producers of the era. Some of the old ranch hands congregated there, and the saddle shop was a hangout for a lot of the local rodeo hands as well as yard hands. While Bill Yeary worked for C. Sloan he spent many an hour at the saddle shop and since we rode to work together, I had to spend the same amount of time there. I did make use of the time, though, and learned to do a passable job of leather work and bought leather from a salesman named Charles Tandy at Hinckley-Tandy Leather Company. The Yards and the Building had smells that were like perfume to me, but I doubt there will ever be a smell to compare with that of a saddle shop like Edelbrock's. The smell of leather, neat's-foot oil, shellac and wool saddle blankets was something out of this world.

After Joe Edelbrock sold out, the shop was owned by Bobby Burnett, A.V. Atkins, Windy Ryon, and J.T. Boothman. It changed ownership so often that I'm not sure who owned it at what time, but it went under these names in a period of three or four years: Atkins-Burnett, Burnett-Ryon, Atkins-Ryon, Atkins-Boothman, A.V. Atkins Saddle Shop, and Boothman Saddlery.

Frank Leddy opened Leddy's Saddle Shop not too long before the flood of 1942. L. White and Sons Boot Shop had been in business a long time before I got to the Yards, but like everything else, didn't last much longer. I bought many pairs of boots from Victor and Louis White when their best boots were something like forty or fifty dollars a pair.

Eddie Caldwell had a small saddle shop in various locations around the Corner and for a time had a shop in the Texas Hotel. In 1945 or '46, Dick Harman went to work for Caldwell. Dick was about the best "stamp hand" (as leather workers who tooled leather were known) around the Corner at any time. Not only was he extremely artistic, he was extremely fast and could make a belt in just a few minutes' time. He was the first stamp hand to use Old English letters on name belts and also the first in our area to stamp scenes as well as flowers on leather. Dick admitted to having a strange past, but talked very little about it. When he did talk he never moved his lips. We accused him of spending some time in prison, but he would only laugh. He did know a lot about steel engraving and his leather designs were extremely similar to the floral designs on paper currency.

I got to know Dick pretty well and we pulled a lot of stunts on people. We would load an ashtray with firecracker powder and wait for somebody to put a cigarette out in the tray. The results could be spectacular if you used a lot of powder. One day Dick blistered his hand badly when he forgot that he had loaded a tray and used it himself. His ashtrays were famous and a lot of victims lured others into Dick's shop just to get them caught.

At one time Dick had a shop on 29th and Ellis. The building was a two-room affair with both rooms used for the shop. One day a victim from some time past put a nine-shot aerial bomb in one room, lit it and shut the only outside door. This type bomb would shoot and send a charge a hundred or so feet in the air where it would shoot again, making a total of eighteen shots. Poor Dick was trapped in the building, which was only about ten by twenty feet. When the door was opened the smoke was so thick that the light bulbs were tiny pinpoints and Dick was on top of a workbench with a couple of saddle blankets over him.

It was in this shop that Leo Murray asked me to show him a .22 pistol I had. I took it in to show him and without looking at it he pointed between my feet, pulled the trigger (bang) and asked, "Is it loaded?" Unfortunately, it was a nine-shot model. I know exactly how the old-timers felt when they were made to dance by the town toughs because Leo put all nine shots between my feet and I was doing my best to keep both of them off the floor at the same time. I never showed Leo a loaded pistol again.

Bob Schwartz and I wired the horn on Leo's pickup to the stoplight switch so that the horn would honk everytime he stepped on the brake. We were the victims of the joke because we sat around three or four hours for him and he never did show up that day. Leo was the world's worst to tease or pull a practical joke but he could not take even the slightest teasing in return, so guess where that put him. He was well over six feet tall and I doubt that he weighed more than one hundred sixty pounds or so. He couldn't stand the name "Slim" and would swell up like a frog and leave if you called him "Slim" or "Cowboy." He would get so mad, we only used this on him when everything else failed. Leo was a top saddle-bronc rider for a few years in the twenties and thirties and had once worked for the Miller Bros. Wild West Show. Leo was inducted into the National Cowboy Hall of Fame in 1987.

So far as the "Wild West" is concerned, the only "shoot 'em ups" that occurred on the Yards were after work or on weekends when Bill Yeary or somebody would use a .22 rifle to shoot some of the thousands of pigeons that roosted around the Building and in some of the sheds. I have seen some of the gamblers wearing pistols around the Corner and they did use them from time to time, but I never saw one used on anybody.

[13]

The Horseplay

Although it may sound like all work and no play, there was a lot of horseplay and fun at the Yards. Some of it was pretty rough but I don't know of any permanent injuries caused by it.

Most men on the Yards were notorious teasers and if a person couldn't take teasing (as I once couldn't) he soon learned to take it or be laughed off the Yards. A bucket of ice water on your bare back while you were sitting in a water trough in hundred-degree weather felt like it would be fatal at the time, but all lived. There were so many practical jokes that it would take a whole book just to list them. I guess some of them were pretty rough but, after all, so were some of the people.

Lots of horseplay occurred in the Building, especially on rainy days when many people were dodging the rain. For several Christmases, we had some pretty violent firecracker fights in the lobby. A bunch of the younger hands, including me (especially me), would stand in the entrances to the lobby and on the mezzanine and throw firecrackers and "Texas Twisters" (which were known as "nigger chasers") into the center of the lobby. If you aimed them just right from the second floor they would sail in one door of Windy Ryon's store and literally push everyone inside out the other door.

We didn't do this very long at a time because some killjoy would get upset and threaten to call the police, and sometimes they carried out their threats, but the halos were all in place when the police arrived. One Christmas in particular, T.A. Nored, one

Dutch Voelkel on "Mike." Photo courtesy Darel Hampton.

of the owners of Nored Hutchens Commission Company who I guess was in his sixties at the time, got real upset and called the police because of the noise. Naturally the guilty parties were at the far end of the Yards doing some important work when the police arrived. There were more firecrackers the next day and guess who was throwing as many as anybody? Mr. Nored himself.

One of the reasons we shot off firecrackers in the Building was that it was far too dangerous to throw them on the Yards. We could have burned the place down in a short time or we could have scared some cattle and either one would have been bad news for the shooters.

A couple of us loaded some cigars with "lady finger" firecrackers because the ordinary cigar loads didn't seem strong enough for us, all they would do was make a faint "pop." When one of our cigars went off, it was just like the movies — we really blew the end off the cigar and made a believer of the victim. We loaded dozens for Windy Ryon, who got a big kick out of giving them to people bumming cigars.

Although I've mentioned a lot about not drinking around the Yards, nearly every Christmas some generous buyer or commissionman would put a bottle of whiskey on one of the windowsills in the lobby. Anybody who wanted a drink was free to have one and when one bottle was gone, another one usually appeared. When the crowd thinned out and only two or three were still drinking, the donor usually picked up what was left of his bottle to keep the hangers-on from drinking it all.

Another event that took place many Christmases was a square dance in the lobby. This was an annual event in earlier days, but not in my time. We did have them several times while I was there. I was a square dance caller at the time and called a few of the dances.

After selling his interest in the old Edelbrock Saddle Shop, Windy Ryon opened his first store in the lobby of the Building about 1946 and had a pretty complete line of sorting poles, whips, ropes, etc., that were used on the Yards. There were a few of the hands who took great delight in grabbing a whip and popping somebody and usually five minutes later they were being popped just as hard as they had popped. This was mostly the older and more "refined" bunch. Some of the people did play a little too

rough and some of them did it too often, but we were unquestio-
nably a unique group.

Anybody could be the victim of a practical joke and at some
time or another everybody fell victim. C. Sloan would wrap up
an old pair of shoes or a hat that he was ready to throw away
and put the package on the fender of his car when he parked at
the Building, then go to an upstairs window to watch and see
who picked up the package. He always got a kick out of this and
did it for several years.

One very prominent commissionman had to go on a long drunk
at least a couple of times every year. One of his favorite pastimes
when drunk was to take off his clothes in the Stockyards Hotel,
get the girls from the hotel to take off their clothes, then sort them
like cattle in the hallway of the hotel. Nearly every event of this
kind was reported to the Yards in a matter of minutes, and quite
often a crowd would gather to watch. After most of these binges,
this man would fire a couple of hands or cut salaries to make
up for the money he spent.

A lot of funny things happened on the Yards, and a lot of
people could tell funny stories, but a natural-born comedian was
Charley Daggett. Most of the funny things he did can't be told
here, but he had the ability to make wisecracks that would break
anybody up. Charley and C. Sloan spent a lot of time together
as bachelors and I've heard that while they were drinking, Charley
would agitate somebody enough to start a fight, then let Sloan
do the fighting. They were good friends throughout their lives.
Charley was about five feet six inches, pretty heavy and I doubt
if I ever saw him without a cigar that was perpetually two inches
long. He always had a pocketknife in his hand whittling wood
into slivers, then snapping off small pieces of the slivers.

One of the best tellers of funny stories was (and still is) Charley
Thomason. Charley had the knack of adding just enough humor
to every story he told to make it hilarious.

Fred Ryon, Windy's uncle, was a pretty good comedian and
could put on a drunk act that would put a drunk to shame. If
he was drawing blood from a cow or doing some other medical
work and a stranger showed up to watch, Fred would start stag-
gering around, mumbling and mouthing, kick over a bucket, and
still accomplish what he was doing. The stranger usually went
away muttering about that drunk cow doctor. Many times, on

calls to the country, his client would tell him ahead of time that he was having company and for Fred to be drunk when he got there. That's all Fred needed to put on a good show for the visitors. More than once people tried to stop him from working on a horse because he was "too drunk."

Bill Jenkins could do a pretty good job of "throwing" his voice. He could stand next to you and call your name with a voice from way down in his throat in such a way that you would swear that somebody a half mile away was calling you. Bill fooled many a stranger with his trick. He showed me how to do it, but I was only able to fool one or two people.

There were several fights during my time, usually caused by a drunk. In the mid-thirties, a commissionman threw a typewriter at another commissionman, who ducked behind a glass door at the right time. The first man cut his arm badly as the typewriter went through the glass. These were both well-known old-timers who were prominent commissionmen.

If a person looked for trouble, he could find it on Exchange Avenue, especially west of Main Street and particularly after dark. Only a small percentage of the people from the Yards spent much time on the west end of Exchange. After dark, the east end was tough enough for most people.

Nearly any kind of gambling could be found in the area. There were several policy wheels (a popular form of gambling) that drew a lot of money from the blacks who worked at the packing houses. Most of the gambling (and there was a lot of it) was the penny-ante type. I have seen a lot of crap games on the Yards on slow Friday mornings. Seeing the money scattered all over the bricks, I learned why my mother wouldn't let me put money in my mouth when I was little. These crap games were slightly illegal, but I never did see a lot of money change hands. "Sheriff" Dagley, the weighmaster at number five scale, was violently opposed to gambling of any kind. I've seen him "come unglued" when someone in the scale house flipped a coin to determine any simple thing.

Sometime about 1952 or '53, Palmetto Polo became a sport for some of the yard hands. Palmetto Polo is similar to regular polo only in that it is played on horseback with a ball and mallet. A ball about the size of a basketball is used and mallets could be nearly anything that the rider felt he could handle. Most mallets had a shaft of palmetto cane and a head of tough rubber.

The head of the mallet was about four inches square and a couple of inches thick. Several of us got involved in playing the game and played, usually at Hardy Tadlock's arena, for several months.

The rules required that the field be marked off in four or five sections with one man from each team working each section. Our group usually followed the rules for five or six minutes at most, then it was just having fun, every man for himself, playing all over the field, trying to knock a ball under a spooky horse to see if you could get the rider bucked off. J.C. Thompson and Afton Allen were the worst when it came to trying to get somebody bucked off and they succeeded quite often. Others who played were J.D. Tadlock, Bob Schwartz, Mike Ward, Wesley Cleveland, and several others. I don't know if I ever saw all of the players at one time because this was during the drouth and we raised so much dust that it was impossible to see the entire field at any one time. Although we were all in excellent physical shape at that time, polo was extremely tiring and we were sore for several days after our first few matches. The problem was that we used muscles that weren't used regularly. Even the muscles in my toes were sore after we started playing and I think my hair was even sore.

Hardy Tadlock had one of the few individually owned roping arenas in the area and all the calf ropers and would-be ropers gathered at Hardy's as often as possible. George Wilderspin, Windy Ryon, and Charley Thomason were others who owned arenas. Calf roping flourished when cattle were cheap and roping calves didn't cost too much, but the sport declined when calves got too high to use for roping. There was always the chance of crippling a calf and if that calf was a high-priced one the cost of roping went way up. Some people would form a club and rent calves to their members for a quarter or so per run.

To give an example of why rodeoing by yard hands was frowned on, Windy Ryon was rodeoing somewhere in Nebraska, I think, when he got his foot tangled in a rope while he was doing something with a horse in the parking lot of a rodeo. The horse ran away, dragging Windy between and around cars. When they finally got his horse stopped, Windy's ankle and foot were badly mangled and the local doctors wanted to take his foot off. Windy's wife, George, was a nurse and had worked for Dr. Clayton the Fort Worth bone specialist, and knew that Dr. Clayton could save Windy's leg. So she traded their car for a pickup, bought a mattress and put it in the back and drove straight through to Fort Worth where Windy's leg was saved, although he had an artificial ankle joint and walked with a limp the rest of his life. Windy continued to rope for several years even though he had the silver ankle. Because he couldn't bend his ankle properly, he had to have his boots made with a zipper in the side so that he could get them on and off.

Windy Ryon and Bill Yeary were about as wild as any two boys could ever be and live to be adults. When they were in their early teens they would tie two lariat ropes together and stretch them between their saddle horns and ride on each side of the street when the black church had finished services on Sunday mornings. It's a wonder they didn't get killed over this, but somehow they made it. Once they were working for Port Daggett on the Lake Ranch at Pecos. Port sold a steer to a cafe owner in Pecos and had Bill and Windy deliver the steer. Daggett didn't care for the cafe owner, so he found a wild steer, loaded him in a pickup and had the boys back up to the door of the cafe and deliver the steer while the cafe was full of customers.

In later years Windy became a solid citizen and donated to a lot of causes, but he kept a few tricks up his sleeve. He got irritated with his church one time because some committee could not decide on the proper color or type of paint for the sanctuary. Since it was stock show time, Windy hired an itinerant painter who painted the "Welcome Stock Show Visitors" signs on store windows and had him paint a religious mural on the wall of the church. Within a very short time a decision was reached by the committee and the church was properly painted by the next Sunday.

[14]

Horses and Mules

The Yards was an excellent place to break horses because a colt spent so much of his time trying to stand up on the bricks that he didn't think too much about trying to buck you off. Several horses were broken on the Yards every year and once they were broken on the Yards they usually turned out to be real good horses and could stand up anywhere. One exception to breaking horses on the Yards was a colt I kept for a while and tried to break. I let George Brock ride him for a month or so and we had him in fair condition, but we were never able to fully break him. He became a rodeo horse and later this same horse was voted in the top ten saddle broncs of the year for three or four years.

Bill Yeary worked for Sloan off and on for several years, starting when he was about fifteen. His last time to work for Sloan was in the mid-forties shortly before I started work full time. Bill was almost a professional visitor. He never saw a person he couldn't talk to and everybody liked Bill. I learned a lot from Bill about meeting and talking to people but it took me a long time to ever be able to do it like he could.

Bill was living in a house on Sloan's place at Saginaw and he and I rode horseback to the Yards many, many times during 1945 and '46 and had a lot of fun doing so. We would saddle up and leave home around five in the morning when it was too dark to see anything and head for the Yards. We would tie our horses to the fence at the southeast corner of Meacham Field and eat breakfast at Joe Grizzard's Skyline Grill, or ride down to the

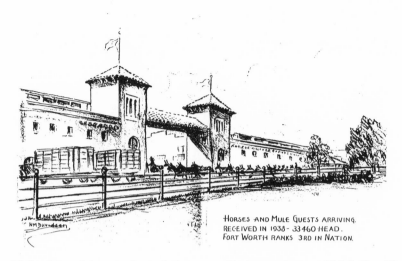

HORSES AND MULE GUESTS ARRIVING.
RECEIVED IN 1938 - 33460 HEAD.
FORT WORTH RANKS 3RD IN NATION.

Mules being driven to the mule barns on Exchange Avenue. N.M. Davidson drawing.

Up-To-Date (which Bill called the out-of-date) Cafe on Main Street just north of 28th Street. It could get exciting riding a "green" horse through the railroad yards between Saginaw and Meacham Field before daylight. Some horses sure didn't like all the banging and whistling of the trains, and they couldn't stand the noise of the airplanes taking off, but after a few trips they would get used to the noise and be able to take anything that would come along.

We would usually turn off North Main just south of Meacham Field and move over a block so we could stay away from traffic. Several Mexican families had moved into the area and one of them had a big German police dog that liked to chase us and bite at our heels (ours, not the horses'). Bill decided we should teach Mr. Dog a lesson, so we bought a couple of long whips and took turns riding a few yards ahead of the other to lead the dog out, then the other would come "whipping and spurring" and work on Mr. Dog with the whip. It didn't take many trips to educate him to sit quietly in his yard when we rode by.

The trip from home to the Yards was eight miles and I don't have any idea of the number of trips we made horseback, but it was quite a few. I remember that in 1945 we heard about FDR's death and the Hiroshima bomb while we were horseback and had stopped for coffee on the way home.

J.A. Tadlock, Sr., was one buyer who was horseback almost every day. This was a necessity when buying bulls because a man on foot could get run over by a bull. Some other buyers rode horses around the Yards, but not on a daily basis. Singles or small pens of cattle could be checked over horseback, but it was wise to check carload lots from the ground. The better buyers did this, but there were some who didn't and they bought a lot of cattle that they shouldn't have.

One of the better known horses was Sam Rodgers horse, Jeep. When Sam whistled for him, Jeep would go looking for Sam no matter how far away he might be. Most of the horses would return to their home pens when turned loose, or they would come when called, regardless of the distance.

For many years Elmer "Dutch" Voelkel rode a white mule named Mike with a Mexican saddle. Mike was about as well known as any human on the Yards. I heard that he lived to be 39 years old. Mike would drive cattle when Dutch went ahead of him lining gates.

One of the more spectacular sights and sounds on the Avenue was to see mules being driven from the mule barns on 25th Street to the barns across the street from the Exchange Building. They usually drove from about fifty to more than a hundred at a time and usually at a run. Several hundred hooves clattering on the bricks make a sound you don't soon forget. This practice died out soon after the war when mules were no longer needed for the military and the demand dropped drastically. Fort Worth was a major mule market for the world. Several foreign governments as well as our own bought thousands of mules through the mule barns at Fort Worth. A large book could be written about the horse and mule trades that took place. Since the mule business was not regulated like the cattle business by the U.S. Department of Agriculture, many a dollar was made in unethical trades and many buyers, including governments, were swindled. The same type trades are taking place today, but with modern military equipment instead of mules. The Turkish government, for one, bought thousands of mules for its army shortly before World War II and several yard hands signed on to go on the mule boats to tend to the mules and get a free trip to Europe.

Some of the better-known horse and mule men that I remember were Wad Ross, Parker Jameson, Darrell Hirsch, Red Yount, Pete Yount, Bobby Burnett and Charlie Team.

Something that may be of interest to the mule fanciers is that Dr. Wilson O. Boaz of Saginaw perfected an operation to "debray" mules while he was in the army in the late forties. Mules could betray a military position by braying at the wrong time. Veterinarians had worked on the operation for many years until Wilson perfected it. Wilson later went with the U.S. Department of Agriculture and came to the Yards several years after I left.

[15]

Braving the Elements

Working on the Yards was nearly all outside work. There were a few pens under sheds, as were the sheep, hog, horse and mule barns, but the dust was much worse in them than outside. There was no stopping for the weather because the work had to go on. You might stop for a few minutes for a hard rain, but the raincoats and suits came out and you went on as if it were a pretty day. This was before lightweight plastic was in use. The good rainsuits were made of heavy rubber that was so hot and caused you to sweat so much that you were about as wet inside the suit as you would be without it. A long rainy spell really messed things up because the Stockyards Company would get behind in its pen cleaning during these times and guess who had to do the honors. You haven't lived until you have to dig twelve or more inches of manure and straw out of a pen and stack it outside in the alley, carrying one fork-full at a time because it was too heavy to throw.

When the brick paving of the Yards had a thin coat of manure and a little rain on it, it was as slick as glass. There was no such thing as a restroom except in the Building and at the drive-in gate. (There were a lot of empty pens, though.) It's just as well, because the smell of the restrooms was worse than the rendering plants. Since I mentioned the rendering plants (a place where dead animals were cooked into grease and tallow), I should explain that the odor that was attributed to the Yards really came from the rendering plants, packing houses and hide factories in the area. This is not to say that the Yards did not have an odor because

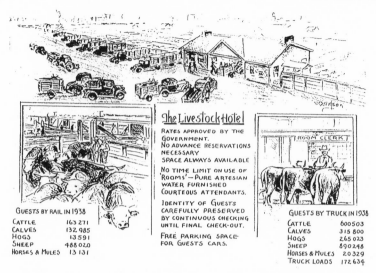

The Livestock Hotel

RATES APPROVED BY THE
GOVERNMENT.
NO ADVANCE RESERVATIONS
NECESSARY
SPACE ALWAYS AVAILABLE

NO TIME LIMIT ON USE OF
'ROOMS'—PURE ARTESIAN
WATER FURNISHED
COURTEOUS ATTENDANTS.

IDENTITY OF GUESTS
CAREFULLY PRESERVED
BY CONTINUOUS CHECKING
UNTIL FINAL CHECK-OUT.

FREE PARKING SPACE
FOR GUESTS CARS.

GUESTS BY RAIL IN 1938

CATTLE	163 271
CALVES	132 985
HOGS	13 591
SHEEP	488 020
HORSES & MULES	13 131

GUESTS BY TRUCK IN 1938

CATTLE	600503
CALVES	315 800
HOGS	265 023
SHEEP	890248
HORSES & MULES	20329
TRUCK LOADS	172634

Trailers arriving at the drive-in gate. N.M. Davidson drawing.

it surely did, but to those of us who were there, it was almost
like perfume. We also had noise pollution. When the pens were
full of cattle, all bawling as loud as they could, a normal conversation was impossible and it was almost impossible to talk on the
telephone closed up in your booth. I will never forget the sounds,
sights, and smells of the Yards. It is still vivid in my memory
and I hope they will stay there always.

In the spring of 1942, there was a fifteen- or twenty-inch rain
one night on the watershed of Marine Creek and the Yards had
a major flood. Water was about ten feet deep at the Corner and
a mule was trapped in the show window of a jewelry store on
the northwest corner of the intersection. Gilbert Winnett and I
were there about noon that day when the mule kicked his way
out. As I recall the mule only had a couple of scratches on him.
Most of the merchants around the Corner were wiped out, losing
all their goods to the flood. I bought several pairs of Pendleton
wool pants and shirts for about a dollar each. When I left the
Yards in '55, there was still a pencil mark on the wall in T.B.
Saunders' office that marked the high-water line in the Building,
14 inches.

At that time, Marine Creek ran under the stock show exhibit
building and several buildings on both sides of Exchange Avenue.
Beginning just south of Hart's Garage on North Main and extend-

ing almost to the present Saunders Park it made a pretty long covered tunnel that soon filled up with trash and caused the water to go around the buildings and flood the area. I don't know how many cattle, sheep, hogs, horses, and mules were lost, but it was quite a few. Soon after the flood, the city of Fort Worth tore down the portion of the exhibit building that was over Marine Creek and that eliminated most of the flood threats. Globe Aircraft Corporation had a factory in this exhibit building during the war, and a lot of surplus equipment was stored on the grounds after the war. Later, there was an automobile dealership in the building.

There were a couple of major fires at the Yards in my time, both of them in the horse and sheep barns. Several small fires broke out on the cattle yards, but none of them were real serious. A fire broke out under our booth one day and even though it was nearly put out when the fire truck came, the firemen took great delight in trying to chop a hole in the floor when all they had to do to get to the fire was climb off the fence. Fire could have caused a lot of damage on the Yards and would have except for everybody being alert to the problem. Barney Seat was the fire marshall for the Stockyards Company and he and several other men patrolled the entire yards with a fire bucket during the dry season. When the manure was dry as powder and the weather was hot, a carelessly dropped cigarette could smolder for hours and then blaze up and be out of control in a few seconds. Smoldering manure has a distinctive odor that can be smelled a long way and we all started looking as soon as we smelled it.

Near every booth was a fire hose and a fire bucket stored in a firebox located on a walkway, so we had plenty of protection available. One cause of fire on the Yards was the practice of throwing baling wire away. Some people had the habit of throwing wire as high and as far as they could, never looking or caring where it went (but hoping it went far enough so they wouldn't be blamed if it hit somebody). When a piece of wire hit a bare electric wire it would put on a fireworks display for a few seconds, and the resulting sparks could set hay on fire. More than once it caused an electric wire to burn in two and fall on cattle and kill them. Lightning also knocked down wires occasionally and killed cattle. Until the late forties the Yards had no city water, but used its own water supply located north of 28th street. When the water had a funny taste to it, we joked (it could have been true) that there was a dead bird in the water line somewhere.

There were a few accidents on the Yards, some serious, most not. Drunks fell off fences several times and were taken to the hospital. There were a few broken bones and lots of bruises and quite a few cuts from pocketknives. One accident that happened shortly after I started working on the Yards was when a steer Horace Winnett was doctoring kicked a jar of screwworm "Smear 62" into his face. "Smear 62" was a pine tar-based medicine that was used to treat screwworm sores. It nearly blinded Horace for a while but he finally got over the problem.

Dr. S.G. Bittick was a veterinarian who was on the Yards for many years. Nearly every booth had some of Doc Bittick's homemade medicines and quite a few of us used them on our own sores and they seemed to work pretty well. He invented a medicine for healing cuts on horses and cattle that he called "Wound (rhymes with pound) Treatment." Because of rationing during the war he couldn't get all the ingredients to make it, so if you wanted some you had to furnish him some of the ingredients yourself. (Mazola oil and mothballs were a couple.) Wound treatment was a fine medicine for cuts or open wounds. It helped a cut "hair over" in a short time.

When he was fourteen or so, Fred Ryon went to work for Dr. Bittick and worked with him for many, many years. Fred never had any medical training, but learned everything Dr. Bittick could teach him plus a lot he discovered himself. Fred was as good a roper (on the ground) as ever lived. Very seldom did he miss. He could throw a loop around a cow's neck and a half hitch around her nose in one motion (making a halter) and draw a sample of blood from her neck before she knew what had happened. It was a show to watch him. Since Fred was not licensed as a veterinarian he was not supposed to take blood samples without Doc Bittick's supervision, so nearly every newly graduated vet who came to Fort Worth turned Fred in to the authorities for some minor infraction. These same vets usually were consulting Fred within a year or so for advice.

Being outside all the time, we had a good view of the airplanes going in and out of Meacham Field. When they took off south from Meacham Field they came directly over the Yards at only six or seven hundred feet, so low that you could almost count the passengers on board. One of the first helicopters I ever saw hovered over the Yards one day while an unknown candidate for the U.S. Senate named Lyndon Johnson asked for votes. We also had a good look at the first flight of the B-36.

Several people on the Yards were pilots during the war and many others learned to fly on their own. Bob Thompson was a carrier pilot in the Pacific and he used to joke that the Japs gave him a medal because he wrecked so many of our planes. Bob Overton flew B-25s in the Pacific and spent a year or so on the Yards before going with Delta Airlines. I heard that he is now retired from Delta. Some of the other pilots on the Yards were Bill Martin (I gave Bill his first ride), Bill Gardenhier, Ed Barnett, Clint Shirley, Sidney Jenkins, Windy Ryon, George Wilderspin, Roy Boswell, and me. Clint Shirley was written up in some national flying magazines for flying directly to ranches in his Aeronca Chief and buying sheep in the late thirties. One of his practices was to fly over a country town and throw out advertising pencils and notebooks. George Wilderspin was an early member of the Civil Air Patrol.

Several years after I had left the Yards, I saw George Wilderspin, Peewee Nix and some others from the Yards at Amon Carter Field, where we watched a couple of hundred big calves loaded into a DC-8 for shipment to South America. It was almost too much for us to comprehend. I remember when a Model T truck could barely haul more than two or three cows. Many times we could load only forty or so yearlings on cattle cars for a week-long trip to Virginia. Now here were a couple of hundred animals on one airplane that would be in Argentina in less than twenty-four hours. I knew that the jets had a lot of power, but it was still hard to believe when the DC-8 made a normal takeoff and was out of sight in less time than it would take to count two hundred head out of a pen. George and I had a long discussion about what the old-timers would have thought of such an event. Certainly most of them would never have believed it.

This story happened before my time on the Yards but it belongs here. One day George Wilderspin took a trip with one of the stockyards pilots to look at some cattle in West Texas. George soon found that he had made a mistake in riding with this particular pilot and told him he wanted out. The pilot told him to hang on and enjoy the trip, but George, being a pilot himself, couldn't enjoy it so he asked the pilot if he was sharp enough to land on a certain road George saw. The pilot said he could do it, and did. When the plane stopped rolling, George got out, told the pilot he would see him in Fort Worth, and walked to a ranch house where he called his wife to come get him.

[16]

The Cattle

The most popular types of cattle that were the most common during the forties were the Herefords, with the Angus or "black muleys" quite a bit behind. The "black baldies" or Hereford-Angus crosses were pretty popular then as now. Brahmans (pronounced by everybody "Bramers," with a long "a") were coming on the scene, but were not nearly as popular as they are now. Santa Gertrudis were also coming on. Charolais were coming up in popularity but were far behind the Herefords and Angus.

Sloan Cattle Company; Walter Graves; Thompson, Tuttle and Thompson; Rodgers and Lane and others handled Herefords and Angus and their crosses almost entirely. Sloan sent thousands of cattle to Virginia, Tennessee, Kentucky, Maryland, Ohio, Georgia, Alabama, Pennsylvania and West Virginia. Rodgers and Lane shipped thousands to the midwest and west. Thompson, Tuttle and Thompson shipped cattle to the east and midwest with a few to California. The California market was not very large at the time and did not come into full force until later when Vann Cattle Company took over as the largest dealer.

Angus cattle are often referred to as "black muleys" because they have no horns and of course are black. Many years ago a couple of ranchmen met a woman whose long-lost brother raised Angus. One of the men knew the brother and in explaining his identity to the other man said, "You know him, he's the man who has the black muleys." The sister, not being from the coun-

89

BATHROOM SCENE
CATTLE BATHED IN ARSENIC
HOGS ———— - CREOSOTE
SHEEP ———— - NICOTINE
GOATS EXEMPT
ALL UNDER GOVERNMENT
SUPERVISION.

N.M.Davidson

Cattle being dipped for ticks. N.M. Davidson drawing.

try, was sure alarmed because she said, "My goodness, I hadn't heard. Is it serious?"

Some dairy cattle came to the Yards, but they went mostly to the packers because there was no dairy cow market as such. Dairies were not as plentiful in those days and there was no great demand for milk cows. There were a few traders who dealt with dairy cows; until the mid forties, there were several traders who dealt in dairy stock and plain cows almost exclusively. Their pens were located on the west side of North Main just south of 28th Street. They had a milk cow market buying and selling a few head at a time to local dairymen or farmers who still kept a milk cow. This area was not a part of the Yards. A few of the traders had been barred from trading on the Yards, but others were honorable men.

There were some memorable shipments to the Yards that I remember. One was a twenty-four-hundred-pound Holstein bull that was sent to the Yards because he had gored to death his owners (two sisters in their fifties or sixties). Several water buffalos were shipped to the Yards, and several cattlo (buffalo-beef cow crosses) showed up as well as a few buffalo. I have seen several mean bulls "walk through" fences as if they weren't there and a lot of Brahman bulls jumped any and every fence they came to.

There were always a few hands who got their horses and caught the cattle that got away. Sometimes these runaways went a lot farther than the North Side. I helped on some of these chases and also got chased by some irate housewives with brooms who didn't like our riding through their yards after the cattle. Dallas Pope, sometimes with his brother Ernest, made good money because the Stockyards Company paid something like five dollars a head to catch the runaways.

Darel Hampton kept a pet steer with five legs that he named George. George had two hind legs joined together on one side from the hip down and another foot on the other leg. Darel got a lot of advertising from George.

George wasn't the only freak on the Yards. I have seen many cattle with an extra leg or two. During the forties, when ranchers with registered herds were trying to breed "blocky" type cattle, they wound up breeding dwarf cattle and quite a few of them were shipped to the Yards. In most cases, the shipper gave a fictitious name so that his herd wouldn't be known for producing dwarf cattle. It was no secret, though; because of the "grapevine" on the Yards, everybody knew who had raised the dwarfs.

Shortly after the war, the Waggoner ranch sent to the Yards several loads of the biggest cattle I had ever seen. The Waggoners had lost most of their cowboys to the war and could not gather the wild cattle until the cowboys returned. Some of the cattle were known to be at least twelve years old and had been hiding on the ranch all that time. A lot of them were as tall as the fences and some of them weighed fifteen or sixteen hundred pounds or more. All of them were sold to the packers.

An interesting note is that most of the larger ranches, Waggoners, Four Sixes, etc., would not allow their cattle to be sold to anyone who was going to keep them in Texas or Oklahoma. This was to prevent cattle with their brands being bought by neighboring ranchers and the possibility of hard feelings developing over proving ownership. At that time, as now, there was not a state-wide brand registration. If a rancher wanted to keep tight control of his brand he registered it in every county in Texas.

[17]

Buyers and Sellers

The yard hands were not the only people who worked long hours. The order buyers and commissionmen had to work as long and, in some cases, longer hours. On a typical day during heavy runs in the spring or fall, an order buyer might leave the Yards in the afternoon and drive as far as two hundred miles to look at one or more loads of cattle, then drive back home and get there in the middle of the night, to be back at the Yards by five-thirty or six in the morning. A commissionman might do the same thing except that his purpose would be to encourage customers to ship their cattle to the Fort Worth Yards instead of elsewhere. If one of these trips was going to include shipping the cattle, usually a yard hand or two went along to help.

Some buyers and commissionmen had ranches a hundred or so miles away that required their attention on a regular basis. The Tadlocks had a ranch at Waurika, Oklahoma, where they sent all their hands nearly every Thursday. In most cases, they would stay there until Saturday and be back on the Yards Monday. But lots of times they would make a quick turnaround and be back Thursday night. It was nothing to drive a hundred or so miles to look at a bunch of cattle every afternoon.

No buyer or salesman would ever admit to belonging to a clique, although they could all point out others who did belong. By "clique," I'm referring to compatibility between a salesman and a buyer. There were several cases where a buyer and sales-man were more friendly and able to deal better than others could.

A BUYER AND COMMISSION
MAN IN ANIMATED CONVER-
SATION OVER A DIFFERENCE
OF '2 BITS' IN THE PRICE
ASKED AND OFFERED.

Salesman on foot is "Uncle Jim" Farmer. N.M. Davidson drawing.

These deals were strictly honest and certainly there was no payoff nor necessarily lower prices, but it sometimes caused some hard feelings. C. Sloan could buy nearly anything he wanted from a couple of salesmen. Joe Lane or Sam Rodgers could do the same thing with other salesmen. This was true with nearly all the buyers and sellers. Some of the salesmen favored the bigger buyers because they had a chance to sell more cattle to them. A few buyers had some ongoing deals with some salesmen that weren't quite ethical. No one really got hurt on these deals, but the ethics were bent out of shape.

For the women who worked in the offices, the hours could be as long as for the yard men. The paper work went along with the yard work and the girls had to stay at night and finish, but they had the advantage of not having to get to work quite as early as the men.

The smaller operators were usually a one-man operation and had to do all the work alone, from going to the country to entice shipments to the Yards, to yarding the cattle, feeding, selling and weighing them, and doing a little of the office work on top of that.

The heaviest weekly runs of cattle always came on Mondays and Tuesdays, then tapered off toward the end of the week. The heaviest annual runs were during the spring and fall, but summer runs were not light. Winter was always slow. When the heavy runs started there would be monumental traffic jams with the trucks trying to get unloaded at the drive-in gate. North Main and 28th Street were main traffic arteries through Fort Worth and if the traffic got blocked it could be bad. Trucks would normally wait their turn on the street that they arrived on, but during heavy runs the police would direct them west on 28th to turn around and form a single line back to the Yards. More than once the line stretched as far as the Jacksboro Highway, and a couple of times I saw trucks as far as Churchill Road in River Oaks. On days like that you could forget all about girls or anything else for some time to come because your days and nights were going to be busy.

[18]

Residents and Neighbors

There were several businesses in the Building that were not directly associated with the Yards. I have mentioned earlier the O.M. Franklin Blackleg Serum Company. Until the early forties, Globe Laboratories had an office in the lobby of the Building where they sold a line of livestock medicines in competition with Franklin. Johnnie Lou Brauner was the secretary. Windy Ryon later opened his establishment in Globe's location.

For several years, feed dealers H.T. Bibb Company and Western Feeders Supply Company had offices in the Building. They did not keep feed in the Building for sale, of course, but acted as brokers for carload lots of feed. Bibb did have a feed store that was located at North Main and 28th for many years. Western Feeders did not have a retail outlet but handled feed contracts.

Burris Mills sponsored Ted Gouldy's popular noon radio broadcast of the market news. For many years this broadcast originated from a room on the second floor of the Building that had been equipped for broadcasting. This broadcast also included the Light Crust Doughboys band for a few years.

Burris Mills had a sound truck that they loaned out to rodeos, reunions, county fairs and such, complete with Ted Gouldy as announcer. Ted used to announce for the Avondale Roundup when it was first started in the late forties. He made me feel pretty good once when he turned the microphone over to me and told me to take over his announcing for the afternoon. From that time on I

The female office force, June 1949 first row: Mary Yeager, Opal Bullard, Ruth Saunders, Hettie Lola Dobkins, Lucy Hart, Corbie Johnson, Carnell Thompson, Frances Machos. Second row: Leo Upton, Louise Dunlap, Peggy White, Gussie O'Neal, Billie Brannon, Connie Myers, Byrnelle Anderson, Eva Mayree Jones, Jurene Lee, Audrey Daley, Marietta Barlow, Annie Wiggs. Third row: Evelyn Thetford, Evelyn Hollingsworth, Sarah Swenson, Esther Cotten, Naomi Bostic, Bonnie Shelton, Elna Popejoy, Lucille Miller, Margaret Tillery, Esther Fay Williams, Judy Bratcher. Photo courtesy Marietta Barlow, identification by Lucy Hart Knox.

The female office force, 1956. Photo by Ed Nelson, courtesy Jewell Kleinecke Tinsley.

was never afraid of a microphone and some people said that I must have been vaccinated with a Victrola needle.

Windy Ryon moved his boot and saddle shop into the Building around '46 or so. At that time he and George Murray were partners in the business. Although George was a good leather worker at the time, he didn't stay long and went to work for Ed Chapman learning to make saddles. Many years later George went to work for Windy as a saddle maker. Windy went on to establish a mail-order business and finally moved to larger quarters in the old Stock-yards Company carpenter shop on North Main. Windy's was a popular hangout and there was always a crowd of yard hands around.

Fred Dumas sold life insurance to a lot of people on the Yards but did not have an office there, although he was around the Building nearly every day. His office was in his coat pocket or he would use any available desk in any available office to fill out applications. If I remember correctly he sold me a policy and filled out all the forms in Texas' (Texas Livestock Marketing Association) office since it was just off the lobby.

All of the major railroads that handled cattle through Fort Worth had offices in the Building, including the Santa Fe, Texas & Pacific, Katy, Missouri Pacific, Rock Island, Cotton Belt and a few others. I think the T.& P. and Katy originated more loads of cattle than the others because their roads went into the South, East and Northeast. The Santa Fe hauled thousands of loads every spring to pasture in Kansas and Nebraska, but the shipments orig-inated in South Texas. I have seen entire trainloads of cattle moving north on the Santa Fe. Bill Wells was agent for the Santa Fe, John Simpson for the T.& P. and I believe Charlie Laue was with the Katy.

Although it wasn't in the Building, the Texas and Southwest-ern Cattle Raisers Association had its main office next door in the coliseum. This was the office not only for the brand inspectors, but also for the whole organization, *The Cattleman* magazine and all. Henry Bell was the secretary at that time and Charles Stewart took over in the late forties. When wrestling first started in the coliseum, the Cattle Raisers still had offices there.

For many years, Western Union and Postal Telegraph had offices in the lobby of the Building, complete with uniformed mes-sengers. Postal went out of business sometime in the late thirties, but Western Union kept its office going until the late forties when they closed and moved to their main office downtown. They discontinued their messenger service in the early forties.

There was a barber shop in the west wing of the Building complete with a shoeshine stand. I believe this was a three chair shop and it stayed busy most of the time. There were several barber shops at the Corner, one on East Exchange, one on West Exchange, one or two on North Main, and I believe there was another at 25th and Main. The walls of Nimmo's shop on West Exchange were covered with heads of all sorts of big game. Bob and Charles Horschler took over this shop and Charles finally closed it in the mid-seventies. The Horschler name evolved pretty easily for the yard hands to Horsecollar. I had known them for several years before I knew their real name.

Clarence Marshall owned a newsstand at the Corner for several years. This was the open-air variety newsstand; it was built along a building wall at the southwest intersection of Exchange and North Main. He had an awning that extended over the sidewalk and it was impossible to get to his stand at shift changing time at the packing houses if it was raining because so many people waited for the buses at the newsstand. At that time I think the Fort Worth newspapers were still selling for two or three cents and a bus ride to town was still a dime. Clarence had a bad leg and walked with a limp, but if you drove up in front of his stand and honked at him he would get the newspapers to you even with buses trying to push you out of the way.

Citizen's Hardware Company was a popular hardware store on North Main just north of the Corner. It was washed away in the flood of '42 and was reopened by its former manager as J.D. Spencer Hardware. Mr. and Mrs. Spencer were real fine people and were liked by all. I still have a model 63 Winchester .22 rifle that I bought from Mr. Spencer just after the war for $40.70. The rifle is now worth about $400.

When the packing houses closed every afternoon around five, Exchange Avenue was crowded with people walking to the Corner to catch a bus. North Main was still a major thoroughfare from North Texas and carried a lot of traffic. Combine the extra buses needed for the packing house employees in the afternoon and the regular traffic on Main, and you had monumental traffic jams on a regular basis. Try riding a horse through all this and it could get a little hairy at times.

We envied the packing house workers sometimes when we heard their five o'clock whistle, knowing that we still had several hours to go on the Yards. I don't know how many were employed at the packing houses at that time, but there were hundreds who walked to the Corner. On Friday afternoons, many of these people stopped at Seymour Drescher's White Front Store to get their paychecks cashed. This was before a bank was handy. Seymour charged ten or fifteen cents to cash a check and I'm sure that he cashed thousands of them over the years.

Quite a few of the Stockyards Company employees lived in the Bridgeport and Chico areas and commuted from there. A man named Harms who drove a hay wagon for the Stockyards Company lived at Chico. He built seats into the back of a truck and hauled passengers for several years. Later, he bought a bus and started a regular bus route from Chico to Fort Worth.

Hart's Garage was a favorite filling station (not service station as they are now called) in the area. It was at the corner of North Main and 26th, except that 26th had not been built at the time. In fact, there was a lumberyard in the middle of the present 26th Street. George and Jimmy Cantrell, as well as Bernard Hooper, ran the station from the late thirties until the sixties. They stayed open twenty-four hours a day and did a big business. Hart's was a favorite place to leave a car when you met a salesman at four or five a.m. to go to the country.

Bill Riddle and Bill Mosley owned the Palace Shoeing Shop on Ellis Avenue. They shod many, many horses in the few years that they owned the shop together. Bill Mosley had been shoeing horses around the Yards for most of his life. He was fairly small, only about five-foot-seven or so, weighing maybe one hundred fifty pounds, but the size of the horse made no difference to him. Bill Riddle was six feet or over and he was big enough to handle any horse. I think they charged about four dollars for shoeing in their shop and five dollars to go to the country. In the late fifties Bill Mosley was charging six dollars to drive to Saginaw and shoe my horse and I thought it was too high.

Joe Grizzard owned the Skyline Grill, which was across North Main from the southeast corner of Meacham Field. For several years Joe stayed open twenty-four hours a day and his place was popular with a lot of stockyards people. Joe also had a lot of noon trade from the Federal Aviation Agency crowd who worked a mile or so away. While eating there at noon we noticed that two or three minutes before the FAA bunch arrived, the jukebox, which was a remote control model with remote units in each booth, would suddenly start clicking as if it were being loaded with (in those days) nickels. Joe discovered that some radio man with the FAA was jamming the radio signal on the jukebox box and causing it to play free music while they were eating.

[19]

Entrepreneurs

One trader who had been raised in East Texas had been a dirt-moving contractor before he got in the cow business. This was in the days of horse- and mule-powered equipment and this man had a pretty big business. The story was told on him that after taking a contract to build a state highway, he bought a new bunch of stakes like the ones the roadbed was being marked with, added twelve inches to the figures that were on the original stakes, then swapped stakes and built the roadbed twelve inches higher than the plans called for. The state engineers figured that they had made a mistake and hired Charlie to remove the extra twelve inches. Needless to say, he wasn't trusted as much around the Yards as other traders. This man had a gift of gab and would stand around the front of the Building and try to catch strangers as they came in and offer to buy cattle for them. Surprisingly, he made some money doing this.

Any time a collection was necessary for flowers or a donation to help someone, Manson Reese always volunteered for the duty. Sometimes it seemed that Manson was collecting every day. I volunteered once to get a blood drive going for a friend and was sure surprised at the number of people who turned me down. That was my first and last attempt to ask for donations on the Yards.

About 1946 or 1947 a man from Kansas City or Saint Louis set up a cattle spraying service on the Yards. He had a custom-made sprayer that was designed to move around in the Yards and drive into pens without much trouble. He also had a sprayer pulled

CATERING DEPARTMENT
MEALS --------- A - LA - CARTE
NO EXTRA CHARGE FOR MEALS SERVED IN ROOMS
FOOD AND SERVICE UNEXCELLED.

Loading up at the hay barn. N.M. Davidson drawing.

by a Jeep that was used for spraying in the country. J.P. Bobo
was the first operator of this service, and since DDT was new
and effective, he sprayed a lot of cattle.

The business looked so good that I bought a sprayer in 1947
and started in business, too. I was not allowed to spray on the
Yards but I sprayed thousands of cattle in the country for stockyards people. I guess I must have been in every leased pasture
within fifty miles of Fort Worth and even sprayed some for Jerry
Ralls as far away as Direct, Texas, on the Red River and DeWitt
Kerr in Archer County. Bill Yeary and I drove somewhere near
Love Field in Dallas to get some of the first DDT that was released
by the Army for civilian use in 1945 or 1946.

I sprayed cattle in every conceivable type of pen. There were
log corrals, pipe corrals, some made of solid cross-ties, also trucks,
railroad cars, barns and even old houses. Jerry Ralls had to take
the sideboards off his truck along with a couple of cars to make
a temporary spraying pen near Direct. This particular trip was
my first time to go through the community of Bugtussle. Even
in 1947 the only store in Direct still had a dirt floor.

About the time I quit spraying, Ab Cooper started a spraying
service. Ab and I were comparing notes recently and decided that
if insecticides were really as bad as they say nowadays, we would
both have been dead long ago. We inhaled DDT, BHC, Toxa-
phene, Chlorodane, Rotenone, 245T and many others by the sack

full. We got burned and blistered by some of them and I know I swallowed a lot of them. I may not be here tomorrow, but I'm still here now.

Yard hands or anyone else on the Yards took on all sorts of outside activities to make extra money. Some would work at the branding chute after their regular work was over. Others would help with cow work on weekends for other traders. One sideline that nearly every yard hand was involved in at one time or another was buying feed sacks. Some traders fed quite a few sacks of cottonseed hulls every week and would collect a lot of empty burlap bags in short order. Used sacks would sell for maybe a nickel each, so the hands would try to buy the sacks so they could make a penny or so per sack. A couple of hundred sacks would bring in two dollars profit when two dollars meant something. The biggest drawback to the sack business was some thief taking your collection of sacks that you had saved up for a month and putting you out of business. Even though we had a lot of honorable men on the Yards, some were not worth killing.

Red Oliver's family owned the Stockyards Hotel for many years and Red managed it for a while in the forties. Red had been a track and football star at Texas Christian University in the early thirties. He was a big man and by the forties certainly didn't look like he could run, but he kept a pair of track shoes in his car and quite often would go into a beer joint and start betting he could outrun any man in the house. After some heavy bets were placed (hardly any on Red) the contestants moved outside, Red would put on his track shoes, take off his pants (he had running shorts on under them) and whether the race was the length of the parking lot or half a city block, nearly every time Red collected the money. Many nights, driving down North Main, I have seen a crowd gathered around the parking lot at some beer joint and thought a gang fight was brewing, but it was just Red outrunning another victim.

There was a small black market operated by a former stockyards man at the corner of North Main and 23rd during World War II. Almost any scarce item could be bought from him, including all kinds of ration stamps. I once bought a hundred pounds of sugar for the mother of a girl I was dating, but unfortunately the sugar didn't sweeten my situation with the daughter, who is now one of the wealthiest women in Fort Worth.

There were several wealthy men around the Yards who made their money in pretty low-down ways. The unfortunate thing is that many of the victims of these men knew in advance what might happen to them, but they stuck their necks out anyway and got caught. It was a sad sight to see a man who had at one time been fairly well off caught in one of these situations and spend the rest of his life paying off the villain.

One of these men was the principal owner of a large commission company and was known to all as a miser. He lent money to a lot of small farmers in West Texas to finance their farming operations. When the farmer couldn't make a payment, the commissionman foreclosed immediately and took over the farmer's land. This man eventually owned a lot of land in West Texas and oil was found on quite a bit of it, but he didn't take any of it with him when he died.

Another man, a prominent horse and mule dealer, would lend money to his employees who wanted to make some cattle trades, then if the deal failed (which it did in the majority of cases) and the trader couldn't pay off his debt, the man would take liens on any property or assets the trader might have. The trader had to spend many years working for the man who loaned him the money trying to work off the debts. This man's activities were quite well known and it was a mystery why he was able to trap so many. Only one man was known to survive dealing with this fellow. He became quite wealthy himself but did not resort to using the methods of his former employer.

All of these men died several years ago and have gone to their reward. Certainly some of them went to Hell and made a lot of people happy by doing so, but there is no need to reveal names. Anyone who was on the Yards knows who these people were and we can leave it there.

[20]

The Trading Game

Let me give an example of a cattle trade. A cattle dealer in Ohio wants a load of steer yearlings to put on his farm or to resell to a farmer in his area. He calls or wires Clarence Sloan, gives him an order for a load of "good to choice whiteface steers, weighing 500 pounds, all dehorned, vaccinated for blackleg, hemo-sep (hemorrhagic septicemia or shipping fever), ship in the next two weeks, not cost over 20 cents, draft on such-and-such bank," or he may tell Sloan to use his own judgment about the price.

The only thing in print here is a telegram. Sloan starts looking on the Yards for five-hundred-pound, good quality whiteface steers. He may find one at one commission company and ten at another, or in some cases he may find a full load of exactly what he is looking for at another company. If he is lucky he can find them in one day, otherwise it could take several days to put a load together. To buy the exact cattle that the customer wants, he has to buy some cattle that do not fit the customer's order. These cattle are sorted off and placed in another pen to fill another order. Perhaps this other pen will fit another customer's order, so Sloan makes a few calls and may be able to move this other load immediately.

Sloan was an expert at making up a load that weighed what the customer wanted it to. He bought cattle with enough leeway in the price to cover the shipping charges and vaccination plus a profit for himself. The profit in those days on a load of cattle was hardly ever over fifty cents per hundredweight, but some addi-

107

TRADING
WHEN THE MARKET IS 'SLOW'
A GOOD SALESMAN GETS OUT
HIS TRUSTY BLADE TO DO
SOME ENERGETIC WHITTLING.
WHY? WE DON'T KNOW.

Buyer on horse is George Scaling, salesman whittling is Charley Daggett.
N.M. Davidson drawing.

tional profit could be made by a weight gain. However, the weight gain couldn't be too much, because the shrink would show up when the cattle were received by the customer, and if he continually got cattle that showed too much shrink in weight he would take his business elsewhere. In the event the type cattle the customer wanted was not available, or the price was too high, Sloan would notify his customer and possibly wait until conditions could be met.

At each of the commission companies, the buyer looked the cattle over and tried to buy them at a price he could live with. There was always a lot of haggling over prices before a selling price was reached. Hardly ever was a pen full or a load of cattle sold for the price the buyer asked. This was all part of the game. By bidding a price for the pen with one or more head at a lower price and maybe one or more others at an even lower price, the buyer could cut the overall cost of the cattle involved and reduce the average price per head. The salesman always priced his cattle higher than he knew he could sell them for, then hoped that he could sell as many as he could at the higher price. Some reasons that a few cattle might be priced lower than others in a pen could be their conformation, size, color, or markings. Hereford cattle were subject to being graded by color and markings as well as other criteria.

Putting a load of cattle together that are uniform in size is as hard as getting their weights uniform, but to look right a load must be uniform in size. One animal that is a lot larger or smaller will stick out like a sore thumb.

When you had your "turn" with a commission company you had the right to try to trade on any and all cattle available. However, if you were buying only calves and the buyer who had a turn following you was buying only cows, you could be dealing on the calves and the cow buyer could be trading for the cows at the same time. If you had several orders and the company had a lot of cattle, you could spend as much as a couple of hours completing your deals.

Although it was frowned on, the practice of tying several owners' cattle together for a trade was widely accepted. For instance: A salesman has ten pens of cattle belonging to ten owners. You make bids of different prices on all the cattle but do not buy any one pen while you are looking. After you have seen all the cattle you and the salesman start dealing on all ten pens; so much for this one and that, and if you sell me five pens at a certain price then I can buy the others at such-and-such. The USDA's idea was that each pen of cattle should be dealt with individually. That was a good idea in theory, but there was no way that it could work in practice.

A salesman might offer at twenty-five cents a pound one or several pens of cattle (not all necessarily belonging to the same owner), all about alike in type and quality, but possibly containing a few cattle that just weren't quite the same. The buyer would bid, say twenty-three cents for the pens with the two linebacks and one motley faced steer out at twenty-two cents and the red-necked one at twenty-one cents, and the seller keeps the cold-blooded one. What happened here is that the salesman sorted cattle from one or more owners into pens of the same general type animals and put them close together to make them look alike and possibly bring a better price. This was also an advantage to the buyer because he didn't have to shop around as much. However, the salesman also tried to sell the outs (the linebacks, red-necks, motley faces and cold-bloods) along with the rest of the pen. After all, the more money the cattle bring, the more often the owner will ship to the same commission company.

Sometimes a salesman would peddle a buyer's bid. That is, he would tell every buyer who came by that he had been bid a certain price, then hoped the new buyer would bid more. Sometimes this was a dangerous practice for a salesman because the buyer whose bid was being peddled might cancel his bid and the salesman would be stuck unless some other buyer was willing to take the cattle.

The buyer, on the other hand, had to see what had happened and bid accordingly, because he had to be able to sell to his customer at the lowest prices. So usually a compromise was reached. After visiting with the salesman a little longer about politics, the weather, his family, football scores or the world in general, the buyer would either say "weigh 'em" or walk off. The salesman might accept the offer and make a sale, or he might swear that he couldn't take such a ridiculous price and never "weigh 'em." If he did this, the salesman might sell the cattle to the next bidder who might be willing to pay his price, or perhaps might cut a little off his asking price and make the sale. He might also show the cattle to several other buyers in the next few hours and if he couldn't get a better offer than that of the first buyer, then he would call the first buyer and agree to "weigh 'em," even though it might be late in the day.

On some occasions, a salesman might call a buyer and tell him that he had one or more cattle that were exact duplicates of the cattle that he had bought earlier in the day and he could weigh them at the same price or maybe quote a lower price. If the buyer needed the cattle and trusted the salesman he might buy them sight unseen. Some buyers saw very few cattle and simply allowed salesmen to weigh 'em to them.

A buyer's bid usually was good all day unless he specifically told the salesman that he had to have the cattle "right now," in which case the deal was or was not made. A salesman was honor bound to not sell the cattle to anyone else who made the same bid as the first bidder. Anyone who violated this rule didn't last very long.

Nothing was written down in black and white. It was always on a person's word that the price would be paid. There were very few disputes over these deals, even though most of the transactions were kept in the buyers' and sellers' heads. When a carload was ready to be weighed, the cattle were driven to number four scale, weighed and turned over to the Stockyards Company to be driven to the shipping division, where a federal inspector looked them over for signs of any disease. Just like the modern bureaucracies, I could never see that an inspector standing on a fence could tell anything about a bunch of cattle on the ground, but they had to have something to do. After the inspector had checked them over, the crew from the branding chute took them to be vaccinated or whatever. The cattle were assigned to a certain pen and that pen number would be used to locate the cattle when they were to be loaded.

Mistakes could happen. A few times that I know of we had loads that were mistakenly put on the wrong cars by the loading crew. These mistakes were pretty hard to correct when the cattle might not arrive at their destination for a week and the shipper might not hear about it for days after that. Sometimes hard feelings arose over these incidents because the cattle that had been switched might be similar to the cattle that the customer had ordered, but a lot lighter in weight.

I never saw any of the old-timers buy cattle in a hurry. I was taught to go in the pen with the cattle, check every eye, every hoof, every ear and see that every hair is in place. Make every animal turn around so that you can see any blemish or lameness. Mentally compare the cattle you are looking at with the others that you are buying. See if they have any missing hair where an auction tag was glued on them. Be sure that they are not stale. Any runny noses or ones that don't feel good? See if they all have the same brand. See if they are colored appropriately. Are there any sand-footed ones? Any with knocked-down hips? Any snakey ones? What will they look like a year from now? Answer all these questions, then make your bid, never at the price that was asked. My wife used to get embarrassed with me when we went shopping and I would bid a salesman on an item rather take the price they offered, but the habit goes a long way back. I still have it and still buy some merchandise a little cheaper.

Because the federal inspectors quit about four or four-thirty (and this was in 1950) any cattle being shipped interstate had to be inspected before the inspectors went home. For this reason, you had to have your cattle in the shipping division before that time even though the railroads might not load out until ten p.m. or later. The branding chute often worked late at night to get cattle ready for shipping.

One hot summer day when we were as busy as could be, we had several loads to ship and to help speed things up, I helped the stockyards scale crew take a load of cattle to the shipping division and showed them to the inspector, the stockyards crew put a "paddle" on the gate, and I drove them to the branding chute to make it a little easier on the branding crew. The cattle cars had been ordered and the railroad called us shortly to tell us that this load had not been inspected and therefore could not be shipped. The result was that we had to get a crew from the branding chute to stop what they were doing and drive the cattle back to the shipping division so the inspector could look at them again while they were in care of the branding chute crew. He approved the cattle, the branding chute crew drove them back to the branding chute to work on them and the bureacracy rolled on.

[21]

Cow Tales

When a cowman says that he is feeding his cattle a pound and a half of cake, it means that he is giving each of them one and a half pounds of cottonseed cake per day. Of course, he is not hand feeding each one the pound and a half individually, but the amount he is feeding in troughs to his entire herd averages out to the pound and a half apiece.

Sometime in the late forties, a young doctor from Dallas, whose name I believe was Edwards, came to the Yards to see C. Sloan about buying thirty or so steers to put on a farm he owned north of Dallas. The doctor said that he knew nothing about cattle, but his wife had been raised in the country and wanted to have some cattle so he was buying them for her. He asked what to feed them and how much. Sloan said that cottonseed cake would be the best for the type cattle he had and that a pound and a half or two pounds per day would be plenty.

After the doctor had had the cattle a couple of months, he called to say that he was having a terrible problem, the cattle were extremely thin and he was now giving them fifteen pounds of cake and they still weren't doing good. Fifteen pounds of cake per head would probably kill them, so Sloan made an emergency trip to the doctor's farm to see what the problem was. The doctor had been giving only a pound and a half of cake to the entire thirty or so steers. When he increased the total to fifteen pounds, the cattle still were getting well under the normal ration, per head. Sloan recommended that the doctor ship the cattle the next day,

Looking 'em over. Photo courtesy Sid Jenkins.

but didn't need to mention that the doctor should stay out of the cattle business. That was one lesson the doctor had already learned.

The doctor was able to pen all the steers, but one jumped out of the pen when they were being loaded on the truck and he was unable to pen him again that day. He asked us for help, so Wayne Stewart, one of our yard hands, and I went to the farm to load the steer and take him to the Yards. The farm was located right in the middle of what is now Richardson, but then was nothing but cotton fields. We didn't take a horse with us because we were assured that the steer was back in the pen and the fence had been fixed. Famous last words. When we drove up to the pens, the steer jumped out and headed in the direction of Garland. Wayne and I took turns driving and walking to keep track of the steer.

After a couple of miles through the cotton fields he was tiring (so were we) because of his condition and we were lucky enough to find a barbwire fence that would stop him. We had a couple of ropes with us, and with Wayne on the fender and me driving we got a rope around his neck, then added another rope for safety. But there we were in the middle of a flat cotton field with no way to load him in the pickup. We saw a road about half a mile from us, and with a couple of ropes around his neck for security, we led the steer to the road with the pickup where we could back in the ditch and load him.

He was pretty upset by this time, but we were wilder than the steer and were able to cowboy him into the pickup. The doctor had driven up about the time we had roped the steer in the middle of the field and watched the rest of the event. This was the first time he had seen anything like this and he commented several times that he thought the Wild West had died many years before, but was glad to see that it was still alive. This job started out to be a simple trip to Dallas to pick up a steer and take him to the Yards, but took a little longer as it was close to midnight by the time we ate, drove to the Yards and unloaded the steer and got home. This was a typical situation where you were sent to do a job and you did it, period. There was no such thing as calling in and saying that you couldn't do the job, or the steer got away or any other excuse, because excuses just weren't accepted.

Although the following story has nothing to do with the Yards as such, I'm including it because it shows that cattle do have a lot of sense even though they are considered to be among the dumbest of animals.

One hot afternoon in August of 1945, Bill Yeary and I were riding our pasture at Saginaw checking a bunch of heifers for pinkeye and doctoring them if necessary. We had roped and doctored a few and started to rope another one that needed attention. This heifer was totally blind because of the pinkeye, but she heard us coming and started to run. We were chasing her, but she was getting close to a stock tank, so we held back because the sound of our horses' hooves on the ground was scaring her and we didn't want her to run onto the dam and maybe fall in the water.

When we held back, we noticed that two other heifers that had left the bunch were running side by side and appeared to be chasing the blind heifer, so we watched to see what would happen. The two heifers were about fifty yards behind the blind one and gaining. The blind one was getting close to a fence when the two suddenly stopped as if they were aware that they were scaring the blind one. The blind heifer hit the fence and stopped and shook her head a few times. At this point, the other two heifers started bawling, as if they were calling the blind one, and walked close to her. After a few more bawls that seemed to calm the blind one, the others got on each side of her and walked her back a quarter of a mile or so to the rest of the cattle. Dumb animals? Maybe so, but not the way I saw it.

"George" the steer with five legs owned by Darel Hampton. Photo courtesy Darel Hampton.

This is only one example of strange things I have seen and heard about cattle, but it is the clearest one I ever saw. If you are around cows for a long time, you can see a lot of strange things and a lot of similarities to human actions. Did you ever watch cows baby-sit? They were doing it long before humans ever thought of it, and doing a good job of it. As many as four or five range cows will leave their baby calves in one area of a pasture with one or two other cows who act as sitters. The cows will graze with the rest of the herd and the sitters will stay close to the calves all day. The mothers will return to the calves in the afternoon and the next day a couple of other cows will do the chores. I never have figured out how the cows pick the sitters and why the calves mind them but it works.

[22]

Inspections, Rules and Regulations

Although government regulations weren't as tough as they now are, we had a lot of regulation by the U.S. Department of Agriculture, the Texas Livestock Sanitary Commission, and the Fort Worth Stockyards Company.

A man named Ruff was the USDA man in charge at the Yards and he was pretty strict in applying the rules. It was his determination whether an individual or company should be barred from trading on the Yards. He barred several men from trading before I got there but I think there were only three or four after I came. W.C. Ball took over after Ruff retired.

The USDA saw that no rules of the Packers and Stockyards Act were violated, and that cattle being shipped interstate were free from disease. The Department was in charge of the market news service that kept tabs on livestock numbers and prices at the major markets around the country. There was a big blackboard on the north wall of the lobby that was used to list this information. The Packers and Stockyards Act of 1921 covered too many things to list here, but basically the act regulated all facets of handling cattle through a public stockyards. As long as I was on the Yards, I don't believe I ever heard of a single animal being quarantined for some disease. A lot of cattle were held because of Bang's Disease (now known as brucellosis), but this was found through a blood test and not from a visual inspection. Certain types of cows or heifers were subject to a Bang's test when being shipped, and if they reacted they were branded with a "B" on

117

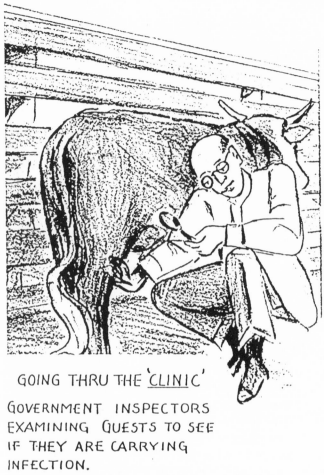

GOING THRU THE 'CLINIC'

GOVERNMENT INSPECTORS
EXAMINING GUESTS TO SEE
IF THEY ARE CARRYING
INFECTION.

Inspector at work. N.M. Davidson drawing.

the jaw and could not be shipped out. Like all rules, many of these could be avoided by shipping from some place other than the Yards, and a lot of people did this at times.

The Texas Livestock Sanitary Commission visually inspected all cattle being shipped anywhere in Texas. This inspection was originally started during the tick quarantine of the twenties and continued many years after the fever tick problem was over, but this is the way of bureaucracy.

Although the Stockyards Company was supposed to have a lot of rules, I think most of those blamed on the company were required by the P&S Act. There were many rules pertaining to buying or selling cattle, how they were weighed, how many could be shipped on a railroad car, how long they could be on a railroad car without being unloaded for feed and water, and on and on.

Since the major packers, Swift and Armour, were major stockholders in the United Stockyards Corporation, they were involved in a lot of the rule making. The packers did not get their buying orders from Chicago until about eight o'clock in the morning and they could not start buying until they had these orders. Since they thought it was unfair for them not to have first chance at buying cattle, there was a rule passed (through the USDA) that no one could buy cattle until after eight in the morning. This was when a siren was installed that went off every morning at eight and told us we could start buying. It may have been at the same time, but I think it was later that the same siren told us to quit buying at three in the afternoon. Although the buying hours were over, the day was far from finished.

There was an organization called the Western Weighers Inspection Bureau (WWIB). According to their rate schedules and tariffs, which were about as complicated as modern airline schedules, the railroads had to charge different freight rates on cattle shipped from the Yards than on cattle shipped from other places. Minimum weights and car sizes were also considered. The WWIB very carefully checked the weights of all cattle shipped from the Yards, and pretty well enforced the rules with an iron hand. Lon Ozee was the WWIB man who checked weights during my time. When he retired he bought the concession stand in the lobby of the Building from "Mrs. Charley," the widow of Charley Richenstine who ran the stand for many years.

To avoid problems and penalties, the bigger order buyers trucked their out-of-state shipments to some nearby railroad loading pens, then shipped by rail from that point. This was a perfectly legal way of getting a better freight rate. C. Sloan shipped hundreds of loads from Arlington (T&P Railroad), Grapevine (MP), and Hodge (Katy). He shipped so many cattle over the Katy that the railroad turned its pens at Hodge over to him and allowed others to use only a few of the thirty or so pens at a time. He also used the Hodge pens to shape up loads that had been bought and trucked in from the country, and thus avoided paying yardage at the Yards.

All cattle and calves that came into the Yards were inspected by brand inspectors who worked for the Texas and Southwestern Cattle Raisers Association. A fee was charged to the shipper for this service and was deducted from the shipper's check. The brand inspectors usually started work about daylight and recorded all brands and earmarks of all the cattle that had come in during the night. Most of the year there were four or five inspectors, but during heavy runs several part-time inspectors were hired.

Henry Bell was secretary-general manager of the Cattle Raisers when I started on the Yards and Charles Stewart took over when Bell retired. Leonard "Goober" Dickson had been an inspector for many years and retired sometime in the mid-forties. George Murray, the Cannon brothers and the Shawver brothers were full-time inspectors for many years. Fred Ryon, Leo Murray and Oliver Ball, among others, were part-time inspectors for several years. Ball was a Fort Worth motorcycle cop at the time and later was a detective captain. All the local market inspectors had deputy sheriff's commissions at the time and the field inspectors, then as now, had Texas Ranger commissions. Charlie Hodges was the first field inspector in the area to have a two-way radio in his car. At that time the entire staff of the TSCRA was housed in offices in the front of the Northside Coliseum.

The inspectors recovered quite a few stolen and strayed cattle as a result of their inspections. In a lot of cases, if stolen cattle were located on the Yards and the thief had not picked up his check, a brand inspector was usually waiting when the shipper came to the office to collect his money.

Some of the unwritten rules that affected everybody and had as much clout as any of the USDA were: Don't intentionally break a lineup. Block a gate or otherwise help if somebody calls for it. Respect another man's turn with a commission company. Be alert for fires and help put them out.

[23]

The Decline and Fall

Many earthshaking events happened during my time on the Yards. Roosevelt died, the Atomic Age began, World War II ended, the Korean War started and ended, jet airplanes became commonplace. The ball-point pen was put on the market. I remember calling all over Fort Worth trying to find one and finally locating one, a Reynolds, at the Kay Drug Company at West Seventh and Penn. So far as I know it was the first one on the Yards. It cost about eight dollars and would write underwater as they claimed because I tried it out in a water trough. Through all this, the Yards operated in the same manner it always had. Although several of us discussed sending a man to the moon someday, we could not see that the end of the Yards was only a few short years away.

There are several schools of thought on what caused the end of the Yards and all of them are partly right. My own opinion is that it was a combination of things, none of which could have been changed and really make any great difference. Its time had come. The Yards had lived its useful life and now it had to make way for the future. The combination of events as I saw it was: The major packers, Swift and Armour, started sending buyers to the country to buy cattle directly from the ranchers and ship them directly to the killing floor. This bypassed the Yards entirely and prevented the Stockyards Company from collecting a yardage fee, it kept the commission companies from making their commission, and it denied some of the traders a profit. Although those fees did not amount to very much per head, when there were lots of cattle that added up to a lot of money.

In addition, the farmers and ranchers who came to the Yards to see their cattle sell found that the City of Fort Worth, in its great wisdom, had put parking meters on every empty parking place anywhere close to the Yards. The Stockyards Company made no effort to cater to the wives of the shippers or see to their comfort. There was a ladies lounge on the second floor of the Building, but no place to sit other than the iron benches in front of the Building, and the Corner was not a very attractive or safe place for the women to visit while the men were on the Yards. All the commission companies had a couch or two in their offices, but that didn't help the situation much. There were no major stores within several miles for them to shop.

Although they wanted the business, too many commissionmen and traders felt the shippers were in their way and really did not want them on the Yards. To cap it off, the Stockyards Company and the commission companies could not foresee the changes that were ahead. Unfortunately, a lot of them acted with the air of the old-fashioned railroad men — that they were all-powerful, could do no wrong and would be around forever. As a result, the railroads and stockyards have just about gone the way of the dinosaurs.

Country people started building auction barns in many little towns and they became a success almost overnight. Farmers and ranchers did not have to haul their cattle long distances to Fort Worth and stand to lose a lot of weight because of shrink. They could take their cattle to the local auction, see them sell, get their check and spend it before they could drive the round trip to Fort Worth.

There is a lot to be said for the auction concept but more, I think, for the central market such as the Yards was. Having spent my time on the Yards, I am still a strong believer in the central market, private treaty sale and think that a person has a better chance to sell there at a better price. The central market offered the farmer or rancher an opportunity to show his cattle to many buyers, who represented a nationwide trade every day of the week. At an auction, a seller has to pick the right day of the week to send his cattle to the sale that attracts the right buyer for his type cattle, and there may be only one or two buyers for the seller's type cattle. If one of the buyers runs out of gas, loses an order or is late getting to the sale, how much competition is there? If the rancher can't sell the cattle that day he must take them home or to another auction on another day.

In any event, the cattle auctions are here to stay. Nowadays, if I want to buy any cattle I have to get somebody to buy them for me because there is no way that I can think fast enough to buy anything coming through the auction ring. While I am making up my mind, they have let the cattle out and are still bidding on them while they run another bunch in.

[24]

Johnny Schwartz, Cowman

There have been a few people in my life that I admired and respected highly. It would be difficult to rate any of these people, but one man right at the top of the list would be Johnny Schwartz. He was an example for a lot of men to follow. Books could be written about him as well as several others on the Yards, but his story is condensed in the following obituary written by Ted Gouldy in the *Stockyards Chatter* for December 1955.

John L. Schwartz, 59, died in a hospital Dec. 7 in Fort Worth. The story of Johnny Schwartz is typical of the kind of career that a young man can build for himself with an humble start as yard man on the Fort Worth Livestock Market.

He came to the Yards as a yard boy with Evans-Snider-Buel. He worked up to salesman and later organized a commission firm with George T. Crowley. Later he was associated with the late J. Quincy Corbett in the commission business. Then he became a dealer and devoted most of his time to his own ranching operations.

He only recently wound up his private ranching operations to devote full time to the job of co-trustee of the vast S.B. Burnett Estate and as manager of the Tom L. Burnett Cattle Company. These far-flung ranch operations cover parts of King, Cottle, Hardeman, Foard and Wichita Counties.

Johnny Schwartz.

His knowledge of the basic cattle business ranged from the daily problems of cowboying to the successful selection of bulls and marketing the crop. He could do it all.

Johnny Schwartz was an intense man. He did everything thoroughly and with complete concentration, whether it was the business of breaking a horse or being friends with a man. There was no middle-ground for Johnny Schwartz. Life was quite simple for him because the answer was always yes or no, do or do not, like or dislike.

This steadfast character coupled with the fact that Johnny Schwartz was one of those rare men who combined fairness with absolute lack of fear, made him a man respected by all and revered by friends.

He is survived by his wife; one son, John Robert Schwartz; three daughters, Mrs. Lindy Berry, Mrs. Joe Reppeto and Miss Nancy Schwartz, all of Fort Worth; four sisters, Mrs. G.W. Bumpers of Idabel, Okla., Mrs. J.W. Bacher of Stillwater, Okla.,

Mrs. R.L. Cobb of Oklahoma City and Mrs. Sim Brauderick of Hazelgreen, Mo., and five grandchildren.

Ted gave a pretty accurate description of Johnny Schwartz. He worked as hard as any man I ever knew and expected anyone who worked for him or around him to do the same. He could not tolerate laziness and as Ted described him, it was "like or dislike." If he liked you, you knew it and if he didn't, you knew that, too. Even men who were not able to keep up the pace working for him, and were fired for one reason or another, still respected him for the man he was.

He, like a lot of other men on the Yards, had an extremely short temper. If he ever raised his voice, it was too late to correct the mistake because "the wreck was on." One time he had taken his family to dinner at Joe T. Garcia's and a couple at a nearby table were feeling the effects of their drinks and started using some bad language. He went to the table and explained that he had his family with him and that he considered the language a little rough for his daughters, and for them to please refrain. (These may not be his exact words, but they will do.) They did hold it down until the meal was over. As the Schwartz family was leaving, the woman at the table made a wise remark to the effect that she hoped the Schwartz girls weren't offended. With that remark, Schwartz grabbed the woman's date and hustled him outside where he explained the difference in good language as opposed to bad and what the results were of making wise remarks around him. Even though it was the man's date who had made the remark, Schwartz settled the affair with the man because there was no way that he would tell a woman what he had on his mind.

One of the greatest days of my life happened one summer when I was helping bale hay on the Schwartz ranch. He was driving the tractor pulling the hay baler and I was stacking bales of hay on a trailer behind the baler. We were baling green cane hay that weighed one hundred-fifty or more pounds per bale and it was a little hard for me to stack hay four bales high as fast as they came out of the baler. Schwartz stopped the tractor and told me to drive and he would stack the hay.

Now I had learned early that you did not complain or make excuses about the work when you worked for Johnny Schwartz, so I had said nothing about the weight of the bales because I needed the job. We traded places and after driving a short distance I noticed that he was not stacking the hay as high as I had been. After we had made one round of the field with him stacking hay, he flagged me down and told me that I had rested enough but that I did not need to stack the hay quite as high as before. I felt ten feet tall after that and could have stacked the hay twice as high because he had found out that I was doing what I had been told to do without complaint.

Epilogue

By 1959 or '60 the Yards that I have written about was gone. An auction was being held a couple of days each week, with private treaty sales on other days. Many of the yard hands that I wrote about had bought the commission companies they had worked for. Others had left the Yards for greener pastures in other parts of Texas or other states. At least a dozen of them moved to San Angelo to expand or start over. A few of these men made fortunes out of cattle, and like always, some lost everything they had.

I don't guess I was ever considered more than a yard hand because I got a yard hand's pay while I worked there. C. Sloan, as well as most of the people on the Yards, was rather conservative and didn't believe in spending much. I did start buying a few cattle about 1949 or 1950. I enjoyed this end of it because it was a lot easier than cleaning pens (even though I still had to do that, too). Daddy was extremely hard to buy for, so I didn't get as involved as I should have. Other buyers could work for him easier than I could, but this is one of the drawbacks of working for your kin. At the time I worked on the Yards I hated the job. I simply could not get used to the idea of so much sitting and waiting. I wanted to build something that could be seen years later and all that I was seeing were empty pens to show for a day's work.

After I left the Yards in 1955 I started building steel barns and corrals. Most of those buildings are still standing and I have the satisfaction that I did build something that would last and could be seen. It didn't take too long to discover that hands are drawing their salary even when it's too wet or cold to work. The construction business was not like the Yards—you can't weld, pour concrete, or do many other things when it is raining. So, I started building steel gates so my crew could work inside. I built a few thousand of them, but I had emphasized quality instead of price, so I came up with a better idea.

One of the barns I built was for Jay Pumphrey, who later became general manager of the S.B. Burnett Estate. When the Estate started developing its race horse program, Jay hired me to build a race horse barn for them at Guthrie, Texas. I spent several months with cowboy labor and did a lot of building for them.

While I was making a four-hundred-mile round trip each week to Guthrie, I spent a lot of time thinking of something that I could build for fifty cents, sell for five dollars, and ship by mail. After a few trips I decided a miniature branding iron attached to a flat piece of wood would make a unique paperweight and would fit the fifty cent/five dollar plan. I built a few of these but my advertising agent threw away the wood and told me to sell steak branding irons. I thought he was silly but in the next ten years I sold over 35,000 of them, making about 25,000 by myself. We were lucky enough to ship them all over the world to the famous and not so famous alike, several presidents, crowned heads of Europe, even a cardinal in the Vatican and many others.

My wife, June, started collecting barbed wire and one day bent a piece of it in a circle and had it gold-plated. You would be surprised how many barbed wire bracelets she sold. I thought, why bend gold-plated wire in a circle? Let's leave it straight and we'll sell it for a swizzle stick. My advertising agent designed a fancy little box to hold six pieces of gold-plated, antique barbed wire swizzle sticks. I bought the plating equipment and before I quit because of the high price of gold, I had plated over ten miles of antique barbed wire. The United States Steel Corporation heard about my work and shipped several rolls of special barbed wire for me to gold-plate for them. I feel proud when I see a set of Swizzle Stix or a brand that I made twenty or so years ago on somebody's coffee table.

There were very few days that I went to the Yards looking forward to anything other than a lot of work. I did what I was told to do and had a love-hate relationship with it. But what I wouldn't give to be able to go back to those times for even a few minutes.

But the Yards that I have written about is gone. A furniture store is located near the old drive-in gate. A night club is in the old stock show cattle barn. Fancy restaurants are in the old stock show exhibit building. The Exchange Building is home to a cafe, offices, art galleries and the like. Poor old number five scale is a rotting skeleton of the past.

Maybe there is a future. I understand that federal government money (that great cure-all) is going to be spent on the area to keep it alive with more tourist attractions, shops, recreational areas, parkways, and so on. Even though there is only a small portion of the Yards left, the spirit of the Yards and the men and women who built it will last always. When I am in the Building it doesn't take much imagination for me to sense the sounds and smells of the past. If you look carefully and with a little imagination you can see C. Sloan leaning against the windows in the back wall of the Building and looking toward the Yards.

Some of it still remains with me. I have a patio built of the same Thurber bricks that I walked on for so long. I have an old double curve rolltop desk that came from the National Livestock Commission Company office. I have scrapbooks filled with items I just had to keep; I have a bench out of a booth (whittling damage and all) refinished and in my living room and many other items including a set of Mike's mule shoes and the water trough plunger that C. Sloan knocked the drunk off the fence with. I have one of the display cases that Windy Ryon had brought from the old Edelbrock saddle shop to the Building. These items mean nothing to anyone else, but there is not enough money in the world to buy them.

In the spring of 1985 I visited with Ab Cooper and later with Bill Addieway and we discussed the idea of having a reunion of all the old hands we could find. I put my computer to work, put out some feelers and with the help of several people including Gary Allen and his office staff, Bill Roach and a few others, we were able to locate over two hundred alumni of the Yards who had worked there before 1960. We had a reunion in November 1985 and had nearly two hundred people attend. At that meeting Bill Roach, Ab Cooper, Hilton Kutch, Patsy Wohler, Bob Chandler and I were appointed to plan another reunion for 1986. We pulled that one off, too, and we hope to continue as long as we can.

Glossary

BELOW THE TRACKS. This is all that is left of the old Yards. A railroad track was used to haul hay to the hay barn and continued through the Yards on across North Main. Anything south of the tracks was "below the tracks."

BOOTH. The wooden buildings that were used as Yard offices. They were built at the owner's expense by the stockyards carpenters. Most order buyers and commission companies had their own. The smaller operators shared. There were usually two or three lockable closets in them, one of them with a telephone. Raincoats, shovels, sorting poles, etc., were kept in them. There was also a water cooler that had to be filled with block ice daily. Electricity was not allowed in any booths other than those used by federal inspectors.

BRANDING CHUTE. The area where cattle were branded, vaccinated, dehorned, or castrated. The branding chute belonged to the Stockyards Company and was leased to individuals who operated it under a tariff set up by the Stockyards Company.

BRINDLE. An animal with stripes running down its sides, like a tiger. This indicated a mixed-breed.

THE BUILDING or EXCHANGE BUILDING. The common name for the Livestock Exchange Building.

BUY. Cattle that a buyer had bought were referred to as his "buy."

CANNERS and CUTTERS. A grade of cows that were too sorry for anything else, used for canned meat.

CATCH PENS. Any small pen. Also a group of small pens where cattle were held after being weighed.

CHOUSE (rhymes with house). A term used in handling cattle a little rougher than necessary. "Don't chouse 'em too much or they'll lose weight."

131

CLEARANCE. A form issued by a commission company or clearing-house authorizing Stockyards Company personnel at the drive-in gate to release cattle to a trucker.

CLEARINGHOUSE. An organization that furnished money, office space and clerical help to traders, order buyers, or commissionmen on a percentage basis. A large commission company or even an individual might act in this capacity. Usually this was a safe business, but it broke C. Sloan in 1929.

COLD BLOODED. This was usually a black-nosed Hereford and was a dead giveaway as to its breeding. Normally, a cold-blooded animal was a Hereford cross with a dairy breed of some type. You couldn't judge an Angus by this sign very easily.

COMMISSION COMPANY. The people who represented the shipper. They were assigned a group of pens at the stockyards where they sold cattle as agents for the owner. A commission company might be only one or two men, or as large as ten or twelve. Their office might be a desk in a corner of a clearinghouse or it might be several rooms with an office staff of six or eight. The commission company sent agents to the country to induce farmers and ranchers to ship cattle to their company. They took care of the owner's cattle, sorted them and possibly grouped them with other cattle to show them better. Their job was to get the best (highest) price they could for their shippers.

THE CORNER. The common name for the area around and a block or so in all directions from the intersection of North Main Street and Exchange Avenue.

COUNTER. The man who counted the cattle off the scales after they were sold and assigned them to pens where they were held for the buyers. A very important position that required some seniority. A slip-up on his part could cost a lot of time.

DIRT ALLEY OR PENS. Some alleys and pens were purposely left unpaved for various reasons. A good place to put sore-footed cattle or ride a young horse that might buck you off.

DRAFT. Any group of cattle weighed at one time, from one head to a scale full. Also a bank draft to pay for cattle.

DRIVER. Anyone who moved cattle around the stockyards. Usually worked for the Stockyards Company driving cattle from the scales to pens.

DRIVE-IN GATE. The truck loading and unloading chutes located, during my time, at the extreme north end of the Yards on 28th Street. The drive-in gate got its name because cattle were "driven in" horseback in the early days. There was a Stockyards Company office on each side of the gate itself. Records of cattle shipped and received were kept here.

DOUBLE HEADER. A pen that was twice the size of a regular pen. A lot of calves were ridden by would-be bullriders in dirt double headers.

DYNAMITE. An animal not nearly as good as the rest of the load, that cost a lot less money. If he could be covered up and sold with the rest he was quite profitable. Buyers had to watch carefully or some salesman might slip one in on them.

FEEDERS. A class of cattle that have just the right amount of fat to go to a feedlot. (See STOCKERS.)

FILL. The weight that cattle gain while on the Yards. Because of the noise and commotion, it was not always easy to put much fill in cattle.

FIRE BOX. A red, wooden cabinet that contained a short length of fire hose that was connected to a water main. There were many of these located on walkways all over the Yards. The fire hoses were sometimes used to spray cattle and cool them off in extremely hot weather.

HAY BARN. A brick building owned by the Stockyards Company to store hay for sale on the Yards. Dan Starnes and Monty Colburn were in charge of the hay barn.

HAY RACK. A wooden platform built over the corner of a pen to store hay.

HIP KNOCKER. A wooden extension added to a fence to make a too-short gate close correctly. It was easy for an animal to bump a hip on one of these and hurt itself.

HORSE BARN. Not to be confused with the horse and mule barns used for trading. It was located just north of the entrance to the present Billy Bob's Texas. It was used to house Stockyards Company horses only.

IN AND BY. Most sorting of cattle on the Yards was done by running them down an alley and catching the sort "in" the pen or "by."

KEYMAN or KEYO. An employee of the Stockyards Company who was authorized to unlock pens on request of buyers or commissionmen. All pens of cattle were locked every night and every time ownership changed. A keyman was always called "Keyo."

LINEBACK. A Hereford with a longer than usual white stripe on his neck continuing behind his shoulders.

LINEUP. Gates set properly to drive cattle for some distance through the Yards. It was taboo to "break" someone's lineup by leaving gates open so his cattle could scatter. On busy days only a short lineup could be made. Late in the afternoon or night one might be made the full length of the Yards.

MANGER. A trough for feeding hay. All mangers and troughs were built into the fences in each pen.

MATCHING. A method of determining the order in which buyers could look at cattle at commission companies.

MOTLEY FACE. A Hereford with spots or other marks on its face. The meat from a lineback, brindle or motley face was as good as any other.

MULEY. A naturally hornless animal, but the term usually applies to any dehorned animal.

ORDER BUYER or DEALER. The people who represented the farmer or rancher in buying cattle on the stockyards. They might act as agents for farmers, ranchers, individuals, or feeders all over the United States. An order buying firm might be one man or several working together and might have several Yard hands working for them. Under the rules of the U.S. Department of Agriculture and the Stockyards Company, an order buyer could only buy cattle when he had an order from a customer. He had to be able to buy cattle for his customer at the best (lowest) price. (Compare this to COMMISSION COMPANY.)

OUTSIDER. Any stranger or non-regular buyer on the stockyards.

PACKER BUYERS. Men who are employed by and buy cattle for packing houses. Buyers for major packers did not buy cattle for anyone else. Buyers for small packers often bought for others.

PADDLE. A wooden slat about an inch and a half wide by six inches long with a piece of baling wire made into a hook on one end and with the words BRANDING CHUTE carved into it. It was hung on the lock of a pen in the shipping division to reserve the pen for cattle being worked at the branding chute.

PLANT. If a trader or order buyer had a few head that he could not dispose of, he would "plant" them with a commission company under a fictitious name for resale. Buyers were real touchy about buying an animal they knew belonged to another buyer, but would buy the same animal from a commission company with no thought about it.

Q SHEDS. Sheds on the east side of the Yards, used mostly by the packers. "Q" scale was located in these sheds.

RED SHEDS. A group of sheds and covered pens along North Main Street in the northwest section of the Yards. Appropriately, they were painted red. They were used by the packers, usually for cattle that had to be held for some time before butchering.

RED NECK. A Hereford with very little or no white on the top of his neck.

SCALE or SCALE HOUSE. The scales as well as the catch pens that belonged to the scales. The scales were housed in a brick building that also housed the weighmaster's office and were popular in the winter because they were the only places stoves and electricity were permitted.

SHIPPER. The owner of cattle shipped to the Yards.

SHRINK. The amount of weight that cattle would lose in shipping or standing around not eating. Most cattle that were bought in the country were weighed, then a three percent shrink was subtracted because range cattle tend to have a lot of fill in them. Even if cattle were hauled a long way under adverse conditions before being weighed the shrink was still imposed.

SHIPPING DIVISION. The area at the extreme northeast section of the Yards where cattle were held before being loaded on railroad cars.

SORTING. Cattle were shipped to the Yards by the truckload and had to be sorted or classified by the commissionman or buyer as to size, breed, weight, color, quality, sex, etc.

SORTING POLE. A wooden pole five or six feet long used to drive cattle. It came in real handy to help turn cattle with a push to the neck or stop them with a tap on the nose, and was easily broken if you weren't careful.

STALE. An animal is stale if he shows signs (matted hair, bald spots where auction tags have been removed, etc.) of having been kept on the Yards for any length of time. A good trader would catch a stale animal behind a gate and comb his hair to prevent the stale look.

STOCKERS. A class of cattle that are kept on pasture, usually through the winter, with a small amount of feed. They do not have enough fat to go directly to a feedlot, but the owner hopes they will when he sells them in the spring. (See FEEDERS.)

STOCKYARDS COMPANY. The common name for the Fort Worth Stockyards Company (division of The United Stockyards Corporation).

TRADER or SPECULATOR. Usually one man who bought cattle that he thought he could resell at a profit to other traders, order buyers, etc. He did not need to have an order to buy any cattle. He might buy cattle from auctions or directly from farmers and bring them to the Yards to resell, or vice versa.

WALKWAY. The wooden walkways that were built on top of fences.

WAYBILL. A card that was filled out by the shipper or trucker when cattle were shipped to the Yards. It gave necessary information such as the commission company, the owner, special instructions, etc.

WEIGHER. The man who worked for the commission company and weighed its cattle. In most cases, the top job for a Yard hand.

WEIGHMASTER. A Stockyards Company man who weighed the cattle. He was in charge of everything that took place in the scale house and his word was law. A weighmaster's job required top seniority.

YARDMAN. Any employee of a commission company or order buyer working on the Yards.

YARDS. The common name for the Fort Worth Stockyards.

INDEX